Ruth and Skitch Henderson's
Seasons in the Country

For the Norfolk Library

Greetings from
Hunt Hill Farm

Ruth + Skitch

Ruth & Skitch Henderson's

Seasons in the Country

GOOD FOOD FOR FAMILY AND FRIENDS

Foreword by JACQUES PÉPIN

Text with Judith Blahnik

Photographs by Lans Christensen
Design by Beth Tondreau Design

VIKING STUDIO BOOKS
Published by the Penguin Group
Viking Penguin, a division of Penguin Books USA
    Inc., 375 Hudson Street, New York, New York
    10014, U.S.A.
Penguin Books Ltd, 27 Wrights Lane, London W8
    5TZ, England
Penguin Books Australia Ltd, Ringwood, Victoria,
    Australia
Penguin Books Canada Ltd, 2801 John Street,
    Markham, Ontario, Canada L3R 1B4
Penguin Books (N.Z.) Ltd, 182–190 Wairau
    Road, Auckland 10, New Zealand

Penguin Books Ltd, Registered Offices:
Harmondsworth, Middlesex, England

First published in 1990 by Viking Penguin,
    a division of Penguin Books USA Inc.

    2   3   4   5   6   7   8   9   10

Copyright © Ruth Henderson
    and Skitch Henderson, 1990
Photographs copyright © Lans Christensen, 1990
Foreword copyright © Jacques Pépin, 1990
All rights reserved

*Grateful acknowledgment is made for permission to
use the following copyrighted works:*
    Bert Greene's apple pie adapted from *The Store
Cookbook* by Phillip Stephen Schulz. © 1988
Phillip Stephen Schulz.
    Sarah Belk's sandwich of spicy marinated beef
adapted from the forthcoming book *New Southern
Cooking* by Sarah Belk, Simon & Schuster, 1990.
    Sheila Lukins's peas in lemon mayonnaise
adapted from *The New Basics Cookbook* by Julee
Rosso and Sheila Lukins. Copyright © 1989 by
Julee Rosso and Sheila Lukins. By permission of
Workman Publishing Co. Inc. All rights reserved.
    Ruedi Hauser's white chocolate cups by per-
mission of Ruedi Hauser of Hauser Chocolatier,
Bethel, CT.

LIBRARY OF CONGRESS CATALOGING
IN PUBLICATION DATA
Henderson, Ruth (Ruth Einsiedel)
    [Seasons in the country]
Ruth and Skitch Henderson's seasons in the
country / Ruth and Skitch Henderson, with Ju-
dith Blahnik ; photographs by Lans Christensen.
    p.   cm.
ISBN 0-670-82604-9
1. Cookery.   I. Henderson, Skitch, 1918–
II. Title.   III. Title: Seasons in the country.
TX714.H46   1990   89-40781
641.5—dc20

Printed in Japan
Set in Meridien
Designed by Beth Tondreau Design

ACKNOWLEDGMENTS

*O*ur first photo shoot for this book was on Saturday, May 7, 1988, the very day Liz Smith opened the Merryall Community Center's season. We cooked for Liz and forty-nine friends, and all the food was lovingly prepared, photographed, and, most important, every morsel was eaten. This was the way it was all through the last occasion in the book, the Einsiedel anniversary dinner in the spring of 1989. One year of cooking, photographing, writing, eating, and enjoying. We thank all who helped with the cooking and "schlepping," and who gave us such pleasure by sharing the meals.

Most of all, our thanks go to Judith and Lans. We feel you both have become our soul mates. The pleasure of working with you, your understanding and respect for us and each other, combined with your patience and seemingly endless energy fueled by passion and excitement, has been a great joy to us.

Thank you, Susan York, for keeping our lives anchored and in order—for giving us the time to let our spirits soar.

Thank you to our daughter-in-law, Sandra; to Sandy Daniels, Mary Ekstrom, and Steve Landon for helping us plan and cook with unfailing enthusiasm.

Thank you, Sarah and Richard Hill, for moving all but mountains to let us celebrate in just the right spot on the farm.

Thank you, Eileen FitzGerald, for making our gardens grow and understanding the need for the "non"-gardens; for being a friend and subtle guide to our children and for taking such special care of our animal family for so many years.

Thank you, Silo gang: Without your holding the fort we could not have gotten "away" to do this book.

Thank you to our farm family—Chris, Michael, Ryan, and Mia DeFelice—for sur-rounding us with energy and life and for all those hugs.

And to Junie Freemanzon in the cottage, our thanks for being ready to jump in and help, and for always being ready to enjoy.

Thank you to Sharon and Jim Hoge, "farm folks" for a while, for coming back often and joining our table.

Thank you, Michael Fragnito, head of Viking Studio Books. Without you, this book would not exist. And our thanks go to Barbara Williams, editor, expert, and caring shepherd through the process of a first book.

Thank you, Beth Tondreau, for your knowing and sensitive interpretation.

And to our good friend Naomi Graffman, thanks for sharpening your pencil and re-membering so much so well.

Finally, thank you to our family—Hans, Sandra, Kythera, Keiran, Heidi, Bill, Sam, and Alex—for being near us and sharing our life and our love for Hunt Hill Farm.

—R.H. and S.H.

I am very grateful to Phillip Stephen Schulz, the late Bert Greene, and Judith Weber for first introducing me to the Hendersons. Ruth and Skitch's combined energy and ardent commitment have had a great impact on my own life. I say thank you to all the Hen-dersons, to my own family, friends, loved ones, and to my colleagues at *Ladies' Home Journal*. In instances too numerous to mention, they were my anchors, buoys, and life-savers during the two years of work on *Seasons in the Country*.

—J.B.

IN MEMORY OF BERT GREENE, WHO LOVED
OUR FARM AND INSPIRED US TO SHARE
OUR COUNTRY LIFE

FOREWORD

I've been a regular visitor to The Silo Cooking School at the Hendersons' Hunt Hill Farm for several years now, but I'll never forget my first trip there ten years ago. I managed to get lost en route, in part because my sense of direction leaves a great deal to be desired, but also because the school's extraordinarily beautiful location in the Litchfield Hills of Connecticut is, as it says in the brochure, "slightly off the beaten track" and so somewhat difficult to find.

As I learned, however, the destination is well worth the trip from almost anywhere. The complex of buildings is a small village in itself, with tiny paths meandering through rows of flowering bushes. In summer months, strawberries, currants, gooseberries, and blackberries abound and the orchards are filled with every imaginable fruit—from black cherries to peaches, apricots, and apples.

It is not surprising that, living in this beautiful setting, Ruth and Skitch should write the cookbook they did. Connecticut is a place where seasons are important; each has its own beauty and each its own appealing food. These recipes follow the seasons, demonstrating the intelligence of cooks who know that the highest-quality ingredients—those with optimum flavor—are selected in accord with Mother Nature.

The book is a blend of sophistication and good, simple recipes. Full advantage is taken of the plenty from their luscious surroundings in recipes that also capture the essence of cosmopolitan New York—so close and yet so far away—and beyond. Much of the food has an international quality that underscores the worldliness of this well-traveled couple.

There are thousands of cookbooks on the market, but there is always room for one like this that comes straight from the heart. The recipes here show a love of nature and a respect for fresh ingredients, whether they be the pork loin that Skitch spit-roasts slowly on the barbecue while he talks to the cows, the just-picked beets from the garden that Ruth cooks until tender and serves simply with red onion slices, or the seckel pears from a nearby orchard that she transforms into a pear butter. Products they don't grow themselves they obtain, whenever possible, from local farmers; sausages, hams, and bacon come from a neighboring pig farmer.

Good, common-sense cooks make use of leftovers, and this is demonstrated here, among other ways, in a delicious potted pâté, made of leftover meat, that is served with crackers. Two other "next-day" dishes, the Virginia French toast and hot sauerbraten sandwich, also make ingenious and creative use of leftovers. There are special gift foods, among them playful sculptured breads that are perfect for giving.

Most important, perhaps, the book reflects the Hendersons' happiness in the kitchen. The element of fun is never forgotten. Covering a broad range of events—from breakfast in bed to a guest-of-honor cocktail party to an Easter Sunday buffet to a firemen's lunch and a splendid lobster dinner—the menus all reflect a great enjoyment of life, an open-mindedness toward cooking, and a deep understanding and thorough knowledge of food. Whether discussing music, cooking, art, or their Connecticut home—all tightly woven components of their life-style—Ruth and Skitch do so graciously. I know you will enjoy, as I did, meeting the entire Henderson family and their neighbors as they come together with Ruth and Skitch to partake of the food—always original, diverse, and flavorful—and share in the happiness of Hunt Hill Farm.

—JACQUES PÉPIN

CONTENTS

HOW WE GOT HERE

We did not go looking for Hunt Hill Farm—it looked for us. In 1967 we were both immersed in a busy urban life. Skitch, as Musical Director of NBC, appeared nightly on the *Tonight Show*, which taped in New York in those days. Ruth was chairwoman of Friends of City Center and an active fund-raiser and drum-beater for the arts. We had just opened a restaurant, Daly's Dandelion, which was a transformation of a neighborhood tavern that had been run by the Daly family for three generations. Mayor John Lindsay tended bar on opening night. It was the talk of the restaurant scene because of its publike atmosphere, its homey food served in generous portions, and its sidewalk cafe. Daly's was fast becoming the early and late stop for notables as well as for our blue-collar neighbors.

Our lives were rooted in the city. Our older child, Hans, attended the Browning School and Heidi, our daughter, was at Miss Hewitt's. On winter weekends we skied in Vermont. Summers were spent in Long Pond, Massachusetts.

But, unbeknownst to us, things were about to change. Early in 1968, our partner in Daly's, George Cothran, was looking for "an acre" of land and a barn where he could exercise his green thumb. We came along for the ride one day and saw a vacant pre–Civil War dairy farm. The strong European character of the barnyard immediately drew us in. Although two silos were still sturdy, this farm looked almost ramshackle, so we left. But we couldn't forget that barnyard. Two days later, we bought it with George to fix it up and rent it out. As an investment.

After that, on Fridays we took off for New Milford, Connecticut, with paint-brushes and scrapers in hand, and began fixing up the old main house. We found helpful, good neighbors: a carpenter, an electrician, and a plumber. In short time, the place became livable and we found our very first summer tenant, Ali MacGraw.

OPPOSITE: *Every day we can look out from our 1836 Barn and enjoy the view of Bear Hill. Here, from the top of Bear Hill, we can see Upland Road and most of the buildings of Hunt Hill Farm.* ABOVE: *From our driveway, the original Upland Road that separated two farms, we can see beyond the old stone wall to the red 1836 Barn.*

Meanwhile, George dug, planted, and transplanted, bringing in trees from all over the state (most of them only four to five inches tall). He discovered endless amounts of hosta, which he separated and used to fill space after space here and there. He planted beans, peas, tomatoes, corn, cabbage, kohlrabi, greens, and okra. And for Daly's Dandelion, he planted hundreds of yellow flowers. By the time our summer tenant showed up, none of us wanted to leave. But a deal's a deal: we left the gardens, the house, the barnyard, and the trees and counted the days until we would be back.

Throughout the summer we came back often and stayed in the tenant farmer's house, now Hunt Hill Cottage. We harvested the beans and vegetables and brought back flowers to Daly's. By then, Ruth had endless ideas about what to do with the houses and barns—too many ideas for George, so he sold us his share.

In the fall, we both loved strolling down the road to the neighbors' huge red barn, where more than forty cows resided. We loved the sounds, the smells, the fresh milk, the newborn calves and barn cats. Those neighbors, the Bostwick family, would eventually give up farming and sell us part of their farm and the huge red barn we loved so much. We call it the 1836 Barn and it's now where we live. By 1971, the old heifer barn had become Skitch's studio. By 1972, we had renovated the main section of the barn and, with an old friend, Louise King, we opened a cookware store in it and called it The Silo. The stables of the barn then became the cooking school and the hayloft an art gallery.

Meanwhile, we were also busy restaurateurs elsewhere. During these same three years, we restored an old rum warehouse in St. Thomas, which became The

ABOVE: *When you approach the farm via the back way, up Old Northville and Crossmon (still dirt) roads, the first sights of Hunt Hill are the horse pasture, stable, the 1836 Barn with its two silos, and the tobacco barn to the left. Fence posts are decorated with flowering kale for a midday feast in the pasture.*

Wooden Horse. We also bought The Bird and Bottle restaurant, an eighteenth-century carriage stop in Garrison, New York, and were deep into plans to open another Daly's—Daly's Daffodil.

We made the rounds of all our concerns during the week and couldn't wait to land back at the farm on weekends. Gradually, we became more and more involved in the town of New Milford and soon grew into being at the farm more often than not. So, in 1972, we gave up our city address and made Hunt Hill Farm, New Milford, Connecticut, our home.

But we did not leave our passion for food and entertaining behind. Ruth remembers both her Einsiedel and List grandparents as avid cooks and gardeners. Her grandfather Einsiedel's garden stretched up the heights of an entire hillside. At the base of the hill was a rock garden and tufts of hearty plants. Farther up were strawberries, raspberries, currants, gooseberries, and the darkest, largest blackberries Ruth had ever seen. Eighty rabbits of several varieties lived in hutches above the terrace of berry vines. Above the rabbits, on top of the hill, were orchards of black cherries, yellow cherries with red cheeks, and light-red sour cherries. There were peaches and apricots and green and purple plums as well.

Grandmothers Einsiedel and List were always cooking, baking, canning, and marinating. There was rabbit in buttermilk and hard-boiled eggs in their shells, steeped in a brine of cider vinegar, sprigs of dill, yellow mustard seed, and black peppercorns. Their cellars were filled with jams, jellies, vinegars, relishes, and fruit compotes in canning jars with handwritten labels. Ruth's favorite was a four-fruit marmalade, which she still makes today. The Einsiedel house was the only one in

ABOVE, LEFT: *The old farm wagon is a fixture in The Silo barnyard.*
ABOVE, CENTER: *A giant maple throws its spring shadow toward the stable and the 1836 Barnyard.* ABOVE, RIGHT: *Daisies, antique roses, bittersweet, and grapevines thrive in The Silo garden.*

Introduction

xiii

the family to survive the war. When Ruth arrived in the United States—on Thanksgiving Day, 1951—two pieces of luggage contained her most precious cargo. One was a large basket stuffed with her grandmother's *Federbetten* (featherbeds). Once opened by customs, it couldn't be closed. The other was a trunk full of plain white restaurant ware. The service for twelve could hardly be lifted and it's still with us today. The same kind of simple ware is now sold in The Silo Store. Customers buy it up constantly.

Food has always been an important support system in Skitch's life also. After bringing him up in the Midwest on Norwegian favorites like mock hare, herring cakes, and Mother Monsen, Skitch's Aunt Hattie took him to the Blue Bird Coffee Shop in Fargo, North Dakota. That long-since-departed café is his first remembrance of gastronomic pleasure. On the menu was roast pork, true mashed potatoes, gravy,

LEFT: *Hunt Hill Farm combines part of the old Anderson and part of the old Bostwick farms. In the upper left is the original Anderson hay barn; to the right is the pond. The carriage house below and to the left is now the pool house, and below it on the right is the Main House. To its immediate left is Hunt Hill Cottage. The set of barns and barnyards below and to the left is now The Silo Store, Gallery, and Cooking School. Across from it is the 1836 House; below are our horse pasture, riding ring, and stable. To their left is the 1836 Barn; the tobacco barn stands below and to the left.*

and blackberry pie. The plate had a blue trim of nondescript flowers, and that homey image as well as the taste of that meal has not left him to this day.

Because he has spent most of his life as a gypsy, food can be and has been a solace for Skitch when things don't go well and a joy when all the musical notes are in place. He has a vast repertoire of restaurants, diners, and coffee shops all over this land where eyes light up when he arrives. Skitch remembers guest-conducting the Memphis Symphony when Count "Bill" Basie was playing a dance date the same night. Bill took Skitch to a rib place (not a joint) and a new world was opened to him. You'll notice that in this book Skitch always is in command when the occasion calls for a barbecue. He has a network of cooking companions from New Orleans to Kansas City to Tulsa to Norfolk to Tampa who share and compare their techniques and ingredients. But, despite exposure to cuisines all over the world, *Rouladen* prepared at home or, if it were possible, a commute for lunch to the Blue Bird Coffee Shop, is Skitch's idea of true Valhalla. And he has not yet forgiven Joe Baum, then of Restaurant Associates, for closing La Fonda del Sol in the Time & Life Building, across from NBC. During the *Tonight Show* years, it was a joy for our whole family to eat beef there, cooked the Argentinian way. The spirit and food were fabulous. Our kids even had birthday parties there.

Skitch is now busier than ever at the helm of his first love, The New York Pops, and guest-conducting all over the world. The Silo Store, School, and Gallery have grown rapidly and demand nearly full-time devotion from Ruth. We have gradually given up our saloons and restaurants. But we certainly haven't given up entertaining. Each season of the year offers dozens of opportunities to have friends over, to eat, be together, and to enjoy the farm. We hope this book will help others, no matter where they live, to enjoy cooking and entertaining as much as we do.

*F*all

*F*all in New England
is in our blood—
that forever-great
feeling that the best
is yet to come.

FALL

It's time to let go of summer. The window over the desk shows a tiny touch of frost at 6:00 A.M. We remind ourselves to bring in the flowerpots; they'll have to get used to living inside. The morning sky is blue. It's going to be warm at lunchtime. We'll get out our best silver and set up a table outdoors. Or we'll take a basket or tray and find a spot in the sun—a stone wall, a tree stump, or a garden chair.

The first leaves turn while flowers are still blooming. Even the impatiens are still brilliant. The seasons meet, and the colors of the zinnias are more intense than ever. The hydrangeas turn green and we cut them and hang them in the tobacco barn to dry. The geraniums and petunias continue to bloom as though summer were still here. Moved inside, they'll bloom through fall and winter.

The harvest season is upon us. Apples and pears abound. There are pumpkins and gourds of all shapes and sizes. We pull up the cabbages, red and green, the last of the beets and carrots, too—all but the collard greens. They love a good frost, as does the flowering kale, which looks as though it has been dipped in paints: purple, mauve, and green.

Out the large window of the great room in the 1836 Barn, there's a mountainside of trees daily changing color. Then the leaves fall and the rains come. We love the sound of rain pounding the tin roof of the tobacco barn, which is filled with drying flowers and baskets of gourds. After the rains, the trees are nearly bare, showing their shapes and casting skeletonlike shadows. Leaves rustle when we walk. Sweaters and parkas come out of summer storage. Skitch mans his tractor. He fills the wagon hitched behind with leaves and fallen branches. Late in the day, he starts a fire in the cooking shed. There's hot cider with cinnamon and Thanksgiving is just around the corner.

PRECEDING PAGES: *A view of the fish pond, where the long-retired horse trailer becomes a storage shed for the children's fishing poles, barbecue equipment, and hockey sticks.* ABOVE: *Another view of the fish pond.* OPPOSITE, TOP LEFT: *An eight-man wooden racing scull that Hans crewed while he was a student hangs above the tobacco barn doors. When the school converted to*

fiberglass sculls and had no use for the old wooden one, we acquired this one for the memories. ABOVE RIGHT: *Bittersweet berries grow wild on the farm, along fences and on vines that climb the silos.* ABOVE: *When we designed the master bathroom in the 1836 Barn, we chose to have this view while relaxing in the bath.*

Fall

3

When our neighbor's cornfield, a short walk down the road, became a field of pumpkins for the first time, people came from all over to see it. What a crop!
OPPOSITE: *After a late fall rain, leaves carpet a path outside The Silo.*

Fall

5

Skitch's October Barbecue

One way to welcome the season is with a barbecue in early fall. We try to do this every year. Sometimes as many as ninety people are on the guest list. The menu varies from year to year, but Skitch always roasts at least one loin of pork. Whatever the guest count, Skitch spends a good part of the day tending coals, basting meats, preparing side dishes, and talking to the cows, who, ironically, seem interested in barbecue. They press up against the fence to watch.

Skitch's theory about today's barbecuing is that we do it not only to treat our palates but to force ourselves to slow down. A good-tasting barbecue takes patience. You must take time in slow measure.

Another must is a good set of tools. Choose the sturdy type with the thick wooden handles. Be sure you include a basting brush. Also, use fireproof oven mitts—the 17-inch sort. To cook this menu, we use a 5-foot spit for the pork, a grill with rotisserie for the chicken, and another small covered grill for the apples.

Spit-Roasted Loin of Pork

o

Fire-Baked Stuffed Apples

o

Honey Lemon Chicken-in-a-Basket

o

Pineapple Slaw

o

Just-Picked Beets

o

Skillet-Fried Potatoes and Onions

o

Swiss Peach Yeast Cake

LEFT: *Once the fires are started, Skitch doesn't leave the barbecue shed. The cows and neighbors come visiting at the gate and the dogs stay at his side all day long. All are attracted by the sound from his radio and the irresistible smell of roasting food.* ABOVE: *After hours of roasting and several minutes of rest, the loin is ready to be taken off the spit.*

LEFT: *The complete meal: from the top, rolls in a basket, coleslaw, beets, apples, pork loin, chicken, potatoes, and peach cake. Fresh carrots, beets, and zinnias complement the buffet.*

Spit-Roasted Loin of Pork

Skitch has made friends with our local butcher, who will cut the backbone of the pork loin in between the ribs for easy serving, and who will even put it on the spit-rod for us.

1 10-pound loin of pork, with bone, trimmed
4 cloves garlic, bruised
   Salt
½ cup prepared mustard (we prefer an ordinary mustard like Gulden's)
¼ cup peach jam or orange marmalade
   Juice of ½ lemon
1 teaspoon chopped fresh marjoram, or ½ teaspoon dried
¼ cup apple brandy or apple cider
1 tablespoon cider vinegar
½ teaspoon freshly ground black pepper

ABOVE: *Ruth collects copper molds and antique cooking tools and skewers. These hang on the original barn siding, which panels our kitchen.*

Place the pork on your rotisserie spit-rod or ask your butcher to do it for you. Rub the pork with the garlic and sprinkle with salt to taste. Combine remaining ingredients in a medium-size bowl and mix well. Coat the pork with ½ cup of this mixture and set aside.

Prepare the coals. Attach spit-rod to rotisserie and spit-roast the meat over medium-hot heat, basting often with remaining marinade mixture, for 3 hours. (If you use a meat thermometer, which we don't, the internal temperature should read 170° F. when the pork is done.) Remove from heat and let stand 15 minutes before carving.

BELOW: *We can't skimp on charcoal for a perfect fiery bed.*

Serves 16.

Honey Lemon Chicken-in-a-Basket

This is the moistest chicken you'll ever sample from the spit. A "spritzer" bottle is the secret (we use the plastic plant-sprayers you can buy in the hardware store), along with the low heat and the long, slow turning. Take the time! Because of the honey in the sauce, the bird will burn if you rush it.

> 3 2½-pound chickens, cut up
>   Salt and freshly ground black pepper
> ¼ cup chopped fresh marjoram, or 1½ tablespoons dried
> 1 8-ounce jar honey mustard
> ¼ cup lemon juice
>   Water in spray container

Place the chicken in a ceramic baking dish and sprinkle with salt, pepper, and marjoram. Cover and refrigerate overnight.

Combine the honey mustard and lemon juice in a bowl. Mix well. Brush the chicken with the mixture; let stand 30 minutes.

Prepare the coals. Place chicken pieces in a wire basket on your rotisserie spit-rod. Attach spit-rod to rotisserie and roast over low heat, spritzing lightly with water every 15 minutes, until juices run yellow when chicken is pricked with a fork, about 2 hours.

Serves 16.

Fire-Baked Stuffed Apples

This will also work in a covered skillet on the stovetop or in a 300° F. oven.

> 16 McIntosh apples, washed and cored
> 32 pitted prunes
> 4 teaspoons sugar
> 4 teaspoons ground cinnamon

Prepare the coals in a covered grill. In the hollow core of each apple, place, in order, 1 prune, ¼ teaspoon sugar, ¼ teaspoon cinnamon, and another prune. Place apples in a large, well-buttered baking pan. Add enough water to come ¼ inch up the side of the pan. Place pan on grill over medium-hot heat. Close the grill cover and bake, adding water when necessary to maintain ¼-inch depth, until apples are tender, about 45 minutes.

Serves 16.

T O P : *Skitch orchestrates his barbecue with the greatest of patience and care. Each task has his fullest attention. While the pork loin turns on one spit, he slowly bastes the chicken, which tumbles in a rotating basket on another spit. He rarely loses any of the good liquid to the fire.* A B O V E : *We snatched these apples from the old tree in the horse pasture before Jupiter and Salome could eat them.*

ABOVE: *After a morning walk up the mountain, Ruth arranged fall leaves and flowers in our collection of crocks and bottles.*

Dried Flowers

Ruth has collected gray-and-blue crocks for many years. Some go back to the time before she and Skitch were married. She uses them outside in summer and in fall fills them with flowers to dry. During the winter months, she brings them inside, where the flowers last into spring.

Meanwhile, tall bunches of hydrangeas and herbs and stalks of grains and wildflowers are hung to dry in the tobacco barn. These are retrieved later in winter to make wreaths, herb baskets, and bouquets for holiday giving.

Skillet-Fried Potatoes and Onions

    1 cup (2 sticks) unsalted butter, cut in small bits
    6 medium onions, thinly sliced
  32 small red potatoes, washed and sliced ⅛ inch thick
    2 tablespoons chopped fresh marjoram, or 2 teaspoons dried
      Salt and freshly ground black pepper

Melt the butter in a large, deep 14-inch skillet over medium heat. Add onions and potatoes and toss to coat well. Cook, turning often, until onions are soft and potatoes are tender, about 1 hour. Add marjoram and salt and pepper to taste.

Serves 16–18.

A B O V E : *The aroma of potatoes, onions, and fresh marjoram cooking on the open fire announces that the meal is almost ready.*

Just-Picked Beets

  16 small fresh beets, washed, tops cut to ½-inch length
    1 tablespoon red wine vinegar
    2 medium red onions, peeled and sliced

Cook the beets with the vinegar in boiling salted water until tender, about 25 minutes. Drain and immediately immerse in cold running water. With the water running, peel away the skins. Slice and arrange on a platter with the onion slices.

Serves 16.

L E F T : *Green tomatoes, put up in summer, make a ready snack, a picnic side dish, or holiday gift.*

Skitch's October Barbecue

Pineapple Slaw

> 2 medium cabbages, shredded
> 6 medium carrots, grated
> 3 medium onions, diced
> 1 large red bell pepper, diced
> 1 fresh pineapple, peeled, cored, and diced (about 2 cups)
> 2 cups mayonnaise
> ½ cup pineapple juice
> 1 tablespoon white wine vinegar
> 1 teaspoon hot pepper sauce
>   Salt and freshly ground black pepper

Combine the cabbage, carrots, onions, red pepper, and pineapple in a large bowl. In a small bowl, whisk together the mayonnaise, pineapple juice, vinegar, and hot pepper sauce. Add to cabbage mixture; toss until well coated. Add salt and pepper to taste. Chill until ready to serve.

Serves 16–20.

ABOVE: *The table is set with some of our favorite dinnerware, each plate with a painting of a cow in the center. Guests sit in the barbecue shed.*

Swiss Peach Yeast Cake

> 4 packages (¼ ounce each) active dry yeast
> 1 cup milk, warmed
> 4 ounces (½ cup plus ½ tablespoon) light brown sugar, firmly packed
> 8 tablespoons (1 stick) unsalted butter, softened
> 3 medium eggs
> 2 teaspoons salt
> 1½ pounds (5 cups) all-purpose flour
> 8 fresh peaches, peeled and thinly sliced
> ½ cup apricot preserves

Dissolve the yeast in the milk in a large-size bowl. Let stand 5 minutes. Add the sugar, butter, eggs, salt, and flour. Mix well until a soft dough forms. Turn the dough out onto a floured surface and knead until smooth, about 8 minutes. Transfer to a lightly greased bowl, cover with a towel, and let rise 1 hour.

Butter a 12 × 16-inch baking pan. Pat dough down into baking pan. Arrange peach slices to cover top of dough. Let rise 1½ hours.

Preheat the oven to 325° F. Place cake in oven and bake until a toothpick inserted in center comes out clean, about 30 minutes. Cool.

Heat preserves in a small saucepan over medium heat until the consistency of syrup. Brush top of cake with syrup.

Serves 16.

BELOW: *Guests pick up their plates and help themselves. Skitch cuts the meat, the chicken is served out of the basket, and the potatoes and apples remain warm in their skillets.*

Skitch's October Barbecue

Picnic on the Mountain

When we are both home, with no shoulds, oughts, or have-tos, we'll take some time to improvise an outdoor meal. One recent day in mid-October, the first bursts of color appeared in the trees that surround our high-grass meadows on the mountain beyond The Silo. We knew that the next day the mowers would come. But on this day, the sky was radiant blue and host to three slow-soaring hawks. We took a plank for a table, packed food in the jeep, and went up the mountain to our favorite spot. We ate our fill that day, then lay back in the grass and watched the hawks soar above.

Virginia Baked Ham with
Sugar-Mustard Glaze

o

Red Bean Salad

o

White Peach Chutney

o

Chili Chutney

o

Apricot Bread Pudding

LEFT: *A rough wooden plank in the hay field holds our late-afternoon picnic. Ruth's wooden plates, ceramic bowls, and wood-handled flatware take extra effort to carry up the mountain (we used the jeep), but they add so much to our enjoyment.* ABOVE: *We follow Isabelle's lead through the fragrant wildflower fields on the mountain.*

Virginia Baked Ham with Sugar-Mustard Glaze

When Skitch came home from a concert in Norfolk, Virginia, with a ham that had been given to him by one of his friends, we popped it in the oven right away to give it a glaze, thinking it would be good snacking. Instead, it became the main course at our picnic the same day.

  1 10-pound mild pre-cooked ham with bone
  ½ cup prepared mustard
  ½ cup dark brown sugar, firmly packed

Preheat the oven to 325° F. Place the ham on a rack in a roasting pan. Brush on the mustard to cover the ham. Sprinkle with brown sugar. Roast 1½ hours. Cool.

Serves 10–12.

BELOW: *A simple and delicious pleasure is ham carved on the board. Save the bone for a terrific stock!*

Red Bean Salad

1½ pounds dried red beans
2 bay leaves
1 teaspoon red pepper sauce
½ teaspoon English dry mustard
   Juice of 1 lemon
2 tablespoons olive oil
1 teaspoon honey
¼ cup chopped fresh oregano, or 1½ tablespoons dried
1 clove garlic, bruised
1 medium red onion, thinly sliced
4 small green Italian sweet peppers, finely sliced in rounds
   Salt and freshly ground black pepper

Soak the beans in water to cover overnight in a large pot. Without draining, add bay leaves and ½ teaspoon red pepper sauce to beans and soaking water. Heat to boiling, reduce heat, and simmer until tender, about 1 hour. Drain and cool.

Meanwhile, in a medium-size bowl, combine the mustard with a few drops of water to form a paste. Add the remaining red pepper sauce and the next five ingredients and whisk until thickened. Remove the garlic clove with a slotted spoon.

Combine the beans, onion, and peppers in a large bowl. Add salt and pepper to taste. Pour the dressing over the beans and toss well. Serve at room temperature or refrigerate until ready to serve.

Serves 8.

ABOVE: *Pears from the neighbor's orchard, a Vermont cheddar with freshly ground pepper, cherry tomatoes from the garden, and yogurt with crushed red pepper were all on hand and added to the spur-of-the-moment meal.*

LEFT: *From the farm below, the road climbs the mountain through hay fields and wildflowers. At the top, the view is worth the trip.*

White Peach Chutney

This is a glorious condiment for ham. You can substitute yellow peaches if the white ones are too scarce or too costly.

1½	cups distilled white vinegar
2	cups dark brown sugar
2	cups finely chopped onions
6	cloves garlic, finely chopped
1	1-inch piece fresh ginger, peeled and finely chopped
½	lemon, sliced and finely chopped
2	teaspoons coriander seed, crushed
3	cardamom seeds, crushed
2	teaspoons yellow mustard seeds, crushed
2	teaspoons cayenne pepper
18–20	fresh white peaches, peeled, pitted, and chopped (about 9 cups)

Combine the vinegar and brown sugar in a large saucepan. Heat to boiling; add remaining ingredients except peaches. Return to boiling and reduce heat. Simmer until mixture thickens, about 15 minutes. Add the peaches, return to a simmer, and cook 15 minutes longer. Pour into sterilized jars, seal, and store in refrigerator.

Makes about 2½ pints.

Chili Chutney

1½	cups distilled white vinegar
2	cups dark brown sugar
2	cups finely chopped onions
4	cloves garlic, minced
½	lemon, sliced and finely chopped
2	teaspoons coriander seed, crushed
3	cardamom seeds, crushed
2	teaspoons yellow mustard seeds, crushed
1½	teaspoons red peppercorns, crushed
18–20	fresh white peaches, peeled, pitted, and chopped (about 9 cups)
1	cup chopped slivered almonds

TOP: *There is always at least one dog nearby, be it at a picnic or on a walk down the road. Here, Isabelle waits for her share of the edibles.*
ABOVE: *Marigolds keep bugs off the last of the cherry tomatoes.*

Fall

18

½ cup raisins
2 medium fresh red chilies, seeded and diced

Combine the vinegar and brown sugar in a large saucepan over medium heat. Heat to boiling and add remaining ingredients except peaches, almonds, raisins, and chilies. Return to a simmer and cook until mixture thickens, about 15 minutes. Add remaining ingredients and return to boiling; reduce heat and cook 15 more minutes. Pour into sterilized jars, seal, and store in refrigerator.

Makes about 3 pints.

Apricot Bread Pudding

Our daughter-in-law, Sandra, and our son, Hans, sometimes join us on the mountain and bring dessert. This pudding tastes great still warm from the oven. For a heartier look and taste, do as Sandra does and slice your bread from a whole loaf. It makes a difference.

3 ¾-inch-thick slices white bread
¼ cup apricot jam
4 slices white bread, finely crumbled
½ cup dried apricots, julienned
6 medium eggs
3 cups light cream or half-and-half
½ teaspoon ground cinnamon
1 teaspoon vanilla extract
½ cup sugar

Preheat the oven to 350° F. Spread each of the 3 thick slices of bread evenly with apricot jam. Cut each slice into ¾-inch cubes. Combine the bread cubes with the bread crumbs and half the apricots in a 1½-quart soufflé or baking dish.

Beat the remaining ingredients together in a medium-size bowl. Pour over the bread mixture. Sprinkle remaining apricots on top and bake until golden, about 40 minutes. (If bread cubes or apricots brown too quickly, cover the dish with parchment paper. Remove paper the last 5 minutes of baking.) Serve warm, at room temperature, or cold.

Serves 4–6.

T O P : *At 15 years old, the always independent Dimitri, our Siberian husky, strolls where he wants to when he wants to. A bell on his collar makes his presence known to the cats and kittens, who dash for cover when they hear him coming.*
A B O V E : *The potter Robert Parrott made this bowl, which we use all the time. His work has added so much to our lives. He created the great number of ''Henderson'' cups that we use every day for almost everything— from serving water and beer to holding toothbrushes in the bathroom or pencils at the desk.*

Sunday Midday Meal in the Horse Pasture

*T*he energy of change was in the air. It was time to celebrate the season and the farm. Friends, neighbors, and their kids all came. We arranged bales of hay in the pasture to use as tables and set them with family silver, Portuguese pottery, and cabbage rose linens. We sat with a full view of the houses, barns, animals, and all the contrasts of fall. Smithfield Ham *im Schlafrock* gave the meal its country character; and, to make things a little fancy, we served a New England seafood mousse torte as well. With the fall changes all around us and the slight extremes in the menu and the table setting, the celebration was almost as exciting as the season.

New England Seafood Torte

o

Ham *im Schlafrock*

o

Carrot Fig Salad

o

Seckel Pear Butter

o

Tomato Marmalade

o

Shortbread Horse Cookies

LEFT: *A table of 48 bales of hay is set with cabbage-rose napkins and the family silver.* ABOVE: *From our pasture dining room we get a great view of the stable and the 1836 Barn. The large basket holds the silver, horse cookies, and chocolates.* RIGHT: *Kale makes a vivid centerpiece. An oversized basket holds the main course, and the pear butter is served in a pitcher. Green tomatoes from a batch of summer put-ups disappear very quickly.*

New England Seafood Torte

This is about as fancy as we ever get. But it is well worth the trouble.

> 3 pounds sea or bay scallops
> 8 tablespoons (1 stick) unsalted butter, softened
> 3 large eggs, lightly beaten
> 1 quart heavy cream
> ½ teaspoon salt
> ½ teaspoon cayenne pepper
> ½ bunch fresh parsley
> 1 tablespoon chopped fresh tarragon, or 1 teaspoon dried
> ½ bunch watercress
> ½ cup tomato purée
> ¼ cup tomato paste
> 5 crêpes (see recipe, page 23)

Preheat the oven to 350° F. Purée the scallops in a food processor until smooth. Add the butter and purée again, scraping bowl often, until well blended. With processor on, add the eggs, then half the cream in a steady stream; process until well blended, about 10 seconds. Transfer mixture to a mixing bowl.

Whip the remaining cream until soft peaks form and fold into scallop mixture. Add salt and cayenne pepper.

Combine parsley, tarragon, watercress, and one-third of the scallop-mousse mixture in the food processor. Purée until blended, a few seconds. Transfer mixture to a separate bowl.

Combine the tomato purée and tomato paste with half the remaining scallop mixture in the food processor. Purée until blended, a few seconds. Transfer mixture to a second separate bowl.

Butter a 10-inch round cake pan that is 3 inches deep and place 1 crêpe on the bottom. Fill 3 pastry bags, each fitted with ½-inch tips, with the scallop mixtures, one mixture for each bag. Pipe a ring of the white mousse around the circumference of the crêpe. Pipe a ring of the red mousse inside of the white mousse. Pipe a ring of the green mousse inside the red mousse. In the center, put a dollop of the white mousse. Place another crêpe on top of the tricolored mousse and repeat the procedure, beginning this time with green, then white, then red, and green in the center. Place another crêpe on the tricolored mousse and repeat the procedure, beginning this time with the red, then green, then white, and red in the center. Place another crêpe on the mousse and repeat as in the first layer, beginning with white. Place the last crêpe over that and repeat as in the second layer, beginning with the green mousse. Firmly tap cake pan on a hard surface to release air bubbles, cover with a buttered sheet of aluminum foil, and place in a roasting pan on the center rack of the oven. Fill roasting pan with enough hot water to come halfway up the side of the cake pan. Bake until a knife inserted in the center comes out clean, about 1 hour. Cool.

To serve, place cake pan in a hot water bath for 10 seconds. Unmold by inverting cake pan onto a serving platter. Garnish with lemon slices.

Serves 12.

Crêpes

    2 medium eggs
    1 cup milk
      Pinch of salt
    1 cup all-purpose flour
    4 tablespoons (½ stick) unsalted butter, melted

Combine eggs, milk, salt, and flour in a food processor or blender and process until smooth. With processor on, add the melted butter. Continue processing 10 seconds more.

Heat a 10-inch sauté pan until very hot. Brush pan lightly with butter and ladle about ½ cup of the batter into the pan. Tilt pan from side to side until evenly coated with the batter. Cook until crêpe is lightly golden. Turn crêpe and cook on other side 1 minute longer. Lay crêpes flat on paper towels until ready to use.

Makes 5–6 crêpes.

LEFT: *A feast for the eye—this tri-colored seafood torte: whipped cream and scallops create the white layers; add watercress and fresh herbs for the green and a tomato purée for the red.*

Sunday Midday Meal in the Horse Pasture

Ham *im Schlafrock*

Im Schlafrock is German for "in a sleeping coat," and refers to any food baked in pastry.

>   4 packages (¼ ounce each) active dry yeast
>   5 cups cold water
>   2 ounces (4 tablespoons) sugar
>   ¼ cup plus 1 teaspoon vegetable oil
>   5 pounds (16 cups) all-purpose flour
>   1 12-pound pre-cooked ham with bone
>   2 egg whites
>   Pinch of coarse salt

Dissolve the yeast in ¼ cup of the cold water in a large mixing bowl. Add remaining ingredients except ham, egg whites, and salt and mix until a soft dough forms. Knead the dough on a lightly floured surface for 10 minutes. Let rest 30 minutes. Separate the dough into 21 balls (each about 6 ounces, or the size of a tennis ball) and let rest another 10 minutes.

Preheat the oven to 350° F. Line a 15½ × 10½-inch baking sheet with parchment. Dry the ham thoroughly and place it on the baking sheet. Roll balls of dough on a lightly floured surface to form ropes 18 inches long. Wrap each rope around the ham, tucking it under so that the ends meet on the bottom. Overlap each rope slightly so that none of the ham shows. Continue this process until ham is completely covered.

Combine egg whites with coarse salt in a large mixing bowl. Beat well and brush the dough with this mixture. Any leftover dough can be rolled out on a lightly floured surface; using a maple-leaf cookie cutter, cut dough and decorate ham. Brush decorations with egg wash. Bake until dough is golden brown, about 1 hour. Serve warm or cold.

Serves 12.

RIGHT: *Pleasure in contrasts! Here, the country ham and the fancy torte make an exciting marriage.*

OPPOSITE, TOP: *Tomato marmalade and pear butter prove to be the perfect accompaniments.* OPPOSITE, BOTTOM: *Carrot salad is a familiar side dish at many outdoor meals, and for good reason. It is robust, will not wilt, and the flavor seems to improve as time passes.*

Carrot Fig Salad

Ruth keeps a small jar of vanilla sugar, which tastes great in this recipe, handy. It's something her grandmother did. Simply put a whole vanilla bean in your cannister of sugar and let it flavor the sugar. Use this sugar and eliminate the vanilla extract. Delightful!

    12 medium carrots, peeled and julienned
        Juice of 3 lemons
     3 teaspoons sugar
     4 drops vanilla extract
    ⅛ teaspoon salt
    ⅓ cup light vegetable oil or peanut oil
     1 12-ounce package small dried figs, quartered
     6 whole figs, for garnish

Place the carrots in a serving bowl. Combine the lemon juice, sugar, vanilla extract, and salt in a small bowl. Whisk in the oil. Pour the dressing over the carrots and toss until well coated. Add the quartered figs and toss again. Garnish with whole figs.

Serves 12.

Sunday Midday Meal in the Horse Pasture

Next-Day Virginia French Toast

This is a comforting reward for the previous day's efforts.

3 medium eggs
½ teaspoon Cointreau
1 tablespoon unsalted butter
2 slices Ham *im Schlafrock*, about ¼ inch thick
1 cup applesauce, warmed

Beat the eggs and the cointreau in a shallow bowl. Melt the butter in a skillet and heat until foamy. Dip the ham, with the crust attached, in the egg, coating both sides. Place in the skillet and cook 2 minutes on each side.

Serve with warm applesauce.

Serves 2.

ABOVE: *There are never too many tomatoes: when we don't eat them fresh, we pickle the green and make marmalade with the red.*

Seckel Pear Butter

You can make this with any sweet pear. But the little seckel pear has a distinct taste. Ruth used a dozen, freshly picked from the orchard on the ridge.

12 seckel pears, washed
⅛ teaspoon ground cinnamon
⅛ teaspoon ground allspice
1 tablespoon Poire William liqueur (optional)

Place the pears in a medium-size saucepan with ½ inch of water. Heat to boiling, reduce heat, and simmer until pears are tender, about 30 minutes. (There will be very little water left.) Put the pears, a few at a time, through a food mill (stems and all) and transfer purée to a serving bowl. Stir in the spices and optional liqueur. Serve warm, cold, or at room temperature.

Serves 12.

Tomato Marmalade

Our daughter-in-law, Sandra, harvested several of her ripest tomatoes for this marmalade. This is her recipe.

4 cups chopped tomatoes
4 cups cored, peeled, and sliced apples
1 lemon, sliced
3 cups light brown sugar, firmly packed

Combine the tomatoes, apples, and lemon in a large saucepan. Heat to boiling, reduce heat, and cook 15 minutes. Add the sugar and continue to cook until mixture attains the desired thickness, about 1 hour. Pour into sterilized jars and seal.

Makes about 1½ pints.

Shortbread Horse Cookies

1 pound (2 cups plus 4 tablespoons) sugar
1 pound, 6 ounces (5½ sticks) unsalted butter, softened

    2 eggs, separated, plus 2 whole medium eggs
2¼ pounds, 4 ounces (8 cups) all-purpose flour
    1 teaspoon salt
    Sugar for garnish

In a large mixing bowl, beat the sugar with the butter until light. Gradually add the egg yolks and whole eggs one at a time, beating well and scraping bowl after each addition. Add flour and salt and mix just until a soft dough forms. Form dough into a ball, wrap in waxed paper, and chill at least 1 hour.

Preheat the oven to 350° F. Roll dough out on a floured surface to ¼-inch thickness and cut with a 6-inch or 3-inch horse-shaped cookie cutter. Place cookies on an ungreased cookie sheet. Brush with the egg whites and sprinkle with sugar. Bake until golden, about 10 minutes.

Makes 24 large cookies.

BELOW: *Since we usurped Jupiter and Salome's pasture for our celebration, Ruth finds a way to honor them at the celebration.*

Cookies are one of the most underestimated, unappreciated pleasures of life. Take them seriously: cookie shops all over America are making fortunes because cookies make us feel good. At parties, you can create a fun and warm atmosphere with cookies baked in a variety of lively shapes. It sets off the occasion; it makes your guests laugh. Men, especially, will want to take the cookies home. It never fails.

Skitch, for example, is a pilot. Sometimes, for relaxation, he'll take off from Danbury and fly to Montreal and back. Many of our friends are also pilots. When they come to dinner, we make cookies in airplane shapes and pipe their call numbers on the wings.

Sandy Daniels, our cookie wizard at The Silo, has even invented a cookie cake—cookies arranged and piled up like a wedding cake. It's great for kids' parties—no plates, no cutting!

There are cookie cutters available in any good cookware store. They come in so many shapes you can have a lot of fun making choices. We stock ninety different cookie cutters in The Silo, and we love to watch customers choose the ones that fit their lives. There are wild and tame animals, hammers, houses, castles, cars, people in all shapes, trains, tractors, boats—you name it. And if you can't find one to fit your life? Well, we know cookie artists who will make their own shapes from cardboard and cut each shape with a sharp knife. However you do it, you'll love having more cookies in your life.

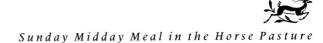

Halloween Party

This is an ideal party if your little ones don't or can't go trick-or-treating. In fact, in this day and age, perhaps a stay-at-home Halloween party is the better choice. Sandy Daniels, director of The Silo Cooking School, helped us put this together for the children and their parents who live nearby. A good time was had by all and there were plenty of treats left over to carry home.

Stew in a Pumpkin
○
Appley Turnovers
○
Old-Fashioned Buttermilk
Doughnuts
○
Pumpkin-Stuffed Oranges

LEFT: *This is a party for children and adults to enjoy together. The hearty stew in a pumpkin is a good main course to serve before everybody dives into the sweet treats.* ABOVE: *Skitch's steam engine is his prized possession and a lure for Ryan, our godson, and his sister, Mia, who live in the 1836 House. It also fascinates Kythera, our granddaughter, and Keiran, our ghostly grandson.*

OPPOSITE, TOP: *Daren Daniels, young son of Sandy and Jack, joins the collection of pumpkins.*
OPPOSITE, MIDDLE: *Kythera, the cat princess, proudly designed her own makeup and also brought the marshmallow treats. Here, she samples the doughnuts.* BELOW *her, Sheba and Isabelle guard the treats.*
OPPOSITE, BOTTOM: *There's never a Henderson party without an appropriate batch of cookies. Here, we served a witch, pumpkin, and cat.*

RIGHT: *Make sure the pumpkin for your stew will fit in your oven. The oranges make good candle holders—we like to send them home as party favors. Cinnamon-stick stirrers flavor the cider.*

Stew in a Pumpkin

Linda Upright Clark taught this recipe in one of our most successful children's classes. When the moms came to pick up their junior chefs, they fell in love with this real-pumpkin tureen.

  3 tablespoons vegetable oil
  1 large onion, roughly chopped
  2 cloves garlic, minced
  2 pounds boneless beef chuck, trimmed and cut into 1½-inch cubes
  2 large tomatoes, peeled, seeded, and chopped
  1 large green bell pepper, seeded and chopped
  3 medium white potatoes, peeled and diced
  3 medium sweet potatoes, peeled and diced
  ¼ teaspoon salt
  ½ teaspoon freshly ground black pepper
  1 teaspoon honey
  2 cups beef broth
  1 medium pumpkin, about 12 pounds (measured to fit your oven)
  1 tablespoon unsalted butter, melted
1½ cups cooked corn, at room temperature
  1 teaspoon chopped fresh marjoram, or pinch dried

Heat the oil in a large saucepan or Dutch oven. Add the onion and cook 1 minute. Add the garlic and cook until onion is soft, about 8 minutes. Transfer to a plate and set aside. Add the meat to the saucepan and sauté until browned on all sides. Add the tomatoes, green pepper, potatoes, salt, pepper, honey, broth, and reserved onions. Heat to boiling, reduce heat, cover, and simmer gently 1 hour.

Meanwhile, preheat the oven to 350° F. Cut the top off the pumpkin and

reserve. Scrape out the seeds and strings and brush the inside with melted butter. Sprinkle with salt and pepper. Place pumpkin on a large ovenproof plate and set it inside a roasting pan. Fill pan with enough water to come just under the rim of the plate. Place the pumpkin top on a separate baking sheet.

Ladle the stew into the pumpkin shell. Bake until shell and top are just tender, about 1 hour. During the last 5 minutes, stir in the corn and marjoram.

Carefully transfer pumpkin (on its plate) to a large platter. To serve, ladle the stew into soup bowls, scooping out some pumpkin meat with each serving.

Serves 8–10.

Appley Turnovers

    4 medium apples, peeled, cored, and diced
      Juice of 1 lemon
    6 tablespoons (¾ stick) unsalted butter, chilled
    ½ cup walnuts, toasted
    ½ cup golden raisins
    1½ pounds (5 cups) all-purpose flour
    1 teaspoon baking powder
    ½ teaspoon ground cloves
    ½ teaspoon freshly grated nutmeg
    ½ teaspoon salt
    1 cup buttermilk
    1 medium egg
    1 tablespoon water

Sprinkle the apples with the lemon juice; set aside.

Melt 2 tablespoons of the butter in a medium-size saucepan. Add the walnuts, raisins, and apples; toss until apples are well coated. Sauté until apples are soft, about 5 minutes. Cool.

Combine the dry ingredients in a large bowl. With 2 knives or a pastry blender, cut in the remaining butter until mixture is the texture of coarse crumbs. Add the buttermilk and stir until a soft dough forms. Form dough into a ball, wrap in waxed paper, and chill 1 hour.

Preheat the oven to 350° F. Lightly grease a baking sheet and set aside. Roll out the dough on a lightly floured surface to a thickness of ⅛ inch. Cut dough into 32 pieces with a 3-inch apple-shaped cookie cutter. Beat the egg with the water to make an egg wash. Brush the edges of each piece of dough with the wash. Place a tablespoon of the cooled apple filling in the

Wild Cat and Fat Witch Cookies

These character cookie shapes were created by Brown Bag Cookie Art, a company in Hill, New Hampshire, that makes fantastic clay cookie molds.

½ cup (1 stick) unsalted butter
5 ounces (¾ cup) sugar
1 large egg
1 tablespoon milk
9½ ounces (2 cups) all-purpose flour
¼ teaspoon salt
¼ teaspoon freshly grated nutmeg
¼ teaspoon baking powder

Beat the butter and sugar until fluffy. Beat in the egg and milk. Combine the dry ingredients in a separate bowl, then gradually stir into the butter mixture. Chill at least 1 hour.

Preheat the oven to 375° F. Fill a lightly floured cookie mold with a small amount of the chilled dough, leveling the top with a knife. Then invert the mold over a lightly greased cookie sheet and tap the mold until cookie dough drops out. Repeat the process until all the dough is used. Bake until edges of cookies are brown, about 10 minutes.

Makes 6–8.

center of each of 16 pieces of dough. Place remaining pieces of dough over filled portions; pinch or press with a fork to seal edges. Prick the tops gently with a fork. Brush with egg wash and place on prepared baking sheet. Bake until golden brown, about 20 minutes.

Makes 16 turnovers.

Old-Fashioned Buttermilk Doughnuts

2 packages (¼ ounce each) active dry yeast
⅓ cup warm water (about 110° F.)
1 teaspoon granulated sugar
1½ cups buttermilk
⅓ cup solid vegetable shortening
2 ounces (¼ cup) brown sugar
2 teaspoons salt
2 teaspoons freshly grated nutmeg
2 large eggs, lightly beaten
1 pound 6 ounces (4½ cups) all-purpose flour
8 tablespoons (1 stick) unsalted butter, softened
1 cup granulated sugar, for coating
1 tablespoon ground cinnamon, for dusting
4 tablespoons (½ stick) unsalted butter, melted

Dissolve the yeast in the warm water with the 1 teaspoon granulated sugar. Let stand 5 minutes, then transfer to a large bowl.

Heat the buttermilk with the shortening in a small saucepan over medium heat until just warm, then add to yeast. Add brown sugar, salt, nutmeg, eggs, and 2 cups of flour, beating well after each addition. Add remaining flour and beat until smooth. Transfer to a lightly greased bowl. Cover with a warm towel and let rise until double in volume, about 1 hour.

Lightly grease a baking sheet and set aside. Punch down dough and place on a lightly floured surface. Pat into a circle about ½ inch thick and cut into shapes with a 3-inch doughnut cutter. Place doughnuts and holes on prepared baking sheet. Let rest, uncovered, for 20 minutes.

Preheat the oven to 450° F. Bake doughnuts and holes until golden brown, about 5 minutes for the holes and 10 minutes for the doughnuts.

Combine granulated sugar and cinnamon in a flat dish with a raised rim. Brush doughnuts and holes with butter and roll them in sugar-cinnamon mixture to coat. Serve hot.

Makes 24 doughnuts and holes.

Pumpkin-Stuffed Oranges

12 navel oranges
½ cup solid vegetable shortening, at room temperature
10½ ounces (1½ cups) granulated sugar
1 cup pumpkin purée
2 large eggs, lightly beaten
⅓ cup frozen orange juice concentrate
8 ounces (1⅔ cups) flour
1 teaspoon baking powder
1 teaspoon baking soda
½ teaspoon salt
1 teaspoon ground cinnamon
½ teaspoon ground allspice
¼ teaspoon freshly grated nutmeg
Spiced whipped cream (see recipe below)
12 2½-inch-long cinnamon sticks

ABOVE: *Kythera's marshmallow cats surround the stuffed oranges.*

Preheat the oven to 350° F. Cut the tops off the oranges and reserve; scrape out the pulp until oranges are hollow. Set aside.

Beat the shortening with the sugar in a bowl until light. Gradually add the pumpkin, eggs, and orange juice concentrate. Sift the dry ingredients together in a large bowl and gradually beat into the pumpkin mixture.

Place oranges in a large muffin tin. Fill two-thirds full with pumpkin batter. Cut a small X through the stem portion of the orange tops and place them on a baking sheet. Bake tops and oranges until a toothpick inserted in the center comes out clean, about 30 minutes. Cool. Ice each with spiced whipped cream, replace tops, and insert a cinnamon stick through the X in the stem portion of the tops.

Serves 12.

BELOW: *We give away the smaller carved pumpkins as party treats.*

Spiced Whipped Cream

1 cup heavy cream
2 tablespoons confectioners' sugar
1 tablespoon pumpkin pie spice

Beat the cream in a large mixing bowl until double in volume. Add the sugar and spice mix. Continue to beat until soft peaks form.

Makes about 2½ cups.

A Family Thanksgiving

*T*his was a rare event: our daughter, Heidi; our son, Hans; his wife, Sandra; and our grandchildren Keiran and Kythera were all on the same coast at the same time! We planned a feast that would allow us to eat and talk in the most leisurely way. Serving platters and bowls sat on a warmer at the end of the table. Once we cleared the soup course, nobody got up for hours. With the food warm and so accessible and the conversation so lively, we relished every minute.

Turkey Place-Card Cookies

o

Pumpkin Soup

o

Baked Cranberries

o

Roast Turkey with Hunt Hill Stuffing and Gravy

o

Steamed Vegetable Trio with Onion-Chestnut Sauce

o

Stuffed Mini-Pumpkins

o

Baked Sweet Potatoes

o

Bert Greene's Apple Pie

o

Pumpkin Pie

L E F T : *Family favorites make the Thanksgiving table a warm and alluring setting for us: Ruth's mother's crystal, a pumpkin from our collection of tureens, pewter and antique wooden utensils, and candlelight.* A B O V E : *"Gesegnete Mahlzeit—guten Appetit—Boom!" We remember Hildegard Einsiedel, Ruth's mother. Since she did not speak English, she said the grace in German. She added the "boom" so that everyone could join in at the end. It was more fun than an "amen." A blessed meal, a good appetite—Boom!*

Turkey Place-Card Cookies

ABOVE: *A gingerbread turkey sits at each person's plate.*

These decorated, edible place markers have become a Thanksgiving tradition with us. They are the first thing to catch the eye and everybody smiles. We use an oversized copper cookie cutter in a turkey shape, from a large collection of animal-shaped cutters available at The Silo Store.

 ¾ cup (1½ sticks) unsalted butter
 5 ounces (⅔ cup) dark brown sugar, firmly packed
 1 teaspoon salt
 1 teaspoon baking soda
 2 teaspoons ground ginger
 2 teaspoons ground cinnamon
 ¼ teaspoon ground cloves
 ¼ teaspoon freshly grated nutmeg
 ¾ cup molasses
 ¼ cup water
15–20 ounces (3–4 cups) all-purpose flour
 3 medium egg whites
 1 16-ounce box confectioners' sugar
 ½ teaspoon cream of tartar

Cream the butter and brown sugar in a large bowl until smooth. Add the salt, baking soda, spices, molasses, and water, beating well after each addition. Gradually beat in 3¼ cups flour until mixture forms a soft dough; add more flour if dough is too moist. Form into a ball, wrap in wax paper, and chill overnight.

Preheat the oven to 350° F. Lightly grease a cookie sheet. Roll dough out on the cookie sheet to a thickness of ⅛ inch. Trim excess from edges of sheet. Using a 6-inch turkey-shaped cookie cutter, cut 4 cookie shapes, 2 inches apart. Remove excess dough from sheet. Bake until lightly brown at the edges, about 10 to 15 minutes. Cool on a rack. Repeat process until all cookies are baked.

Meanwhile, beat the egg whites until foamy. Beat in the confectioners' sugar and cream of tartar and continue beating until thick and smooth. Place mixture in a pastry bag fitted with a fine tip and decorate each cookie according to whim, making sure the name of your guest or loved one appears on the cookie.

Makes 10 large cookies.

Pumpkin Soup

    3 strips lean bacon
    1 tablespoon unsalted butter
    2 medium onions, finely chopped
    1 small pumpkin, seeded, scraped, peeled, and chopped into
          2-inch cubes (about 8 cups)
       Salt and freshly ground black pepper

Sauté the bacon in a large saucepan or Dutch oven over medium heat until crisp. Drain on a paper towel and set aside. Melt the butter in the same pot over medium heat. Add the onions and cook until soft, about 5 minutes. Add the pumpkin and enough water to cover. Heat to boiling, reduce heat, and simmer until pumpkin is tender, about 50 minutes.

Purée the soup in batches in a food processor or blender, being very careful because hot liquid will expand. Transfer the puréed soup to another large pot. Crumble the reserved bacon and add to soup. Heat to boiling, reduce heat, and simmer 15 minutes. Add salt and pepper to taste. Serve immediately.

Serves 8–10.

ABOVE: *Sandra and Ruth shared the job of cooking for the feast. Sandra made the soup and served it garnished with nutmeg and a bay leaf.*

Baked Cranberries

This is easily done a day in advance and heated at the last minute in the microwave. We do prefer to serve it hot.

    4 cups fresh cranberries, washed and picked over
    1 orange (including peel), diced
 1¼ cups dark brown sugar
    1 cup granulated sugar
    2 cinnamon sticks
    6 whole cloves
  ½ cup water

Preheat the oven to 300° F. Combine all ingredients except water in a bean pot or ovenproof casserole and mix well. Make a well in the middle of the berry mixture and pour the water into the well. Bake until berries are tender and mixture is bubbly and the consistency of a thick sauce, about 2 hours.

Serves 8–10.

Roast Turkey with Hunt Hill Stuffing and Gravy

We ordered our turkey ahead of time, picked it up, brought it home, and on Thanksgiving morning discovered it had a wing missing! Poor bird. However, when the moment came to parade the turkey to the table, we camouflaged the wingless side with a generous branch of bay leaves and an arrangement of sweet potatoes and stuffed pumpkins.

<table>
<tr><td>1</td><td>fresh turkey, 17–20 pounds</td></tr>
<tr><td>1</td><td>carrot</td></tr>
<tr><td>1</td><td>stalk celery</td></tr>
<tr><td>1</td><td>onion, peeled</td></tr>
<tr><td>1</td><td>bay leaf</td></tr>
<tr><td>2½</td><td>quarts water</td></tr>
<tr><td></td><td>Salt and freshly ground black pepper</td></tr>
</table>

<table>
<tr><td>9</td><td>slices white bread, cubed</td></tr>
<tr><td>2</td><td>slices pumpernickel bread, toasted and crumbled</td></tr>
<tr><td>3½</td><td>cups dry bread crumbs</td></tr>
<tr><td>1</td><td>cup diced ham (we prefer Westphalian)</td></tr>
<tr><td>1</td><td>cup diced celery</td></tr>
<tr><td>1</td><td>teaspoon dried sage</td></tr>
<tr><td>2</td><td>teaspoons dried marjoram, divided</td></tr>
<tr><td></td><td>Salt and freshly ground black pepper</td></tr>
</table>

<table>
<tr><td>8</td><td>tablespoons (1 stick) unsalted butter, melted, plus 2 tablespoons at room temperature</td></tr>
<tr><td>3</td><td>tablespoons all-purpose flour</td></tr>
<tr><td></td><td>Fresh parsley, for garnish</td></tr>
</table>

Remove giblets from the turkey and place them (without the liver) in a large saucepan. Add the carrot, celery, onion, bay leaf, water, and salt and pepper to taste. Heat to boiling, reduce heat, and simmer until stock is reduced to 5½ cups. Strain and reserve both stock and vegetables.

Preheat the oven to 400° F. To make the stuffing, combine the bread cubes, bread crumbs, ham, celery, sage, 1 teaspoon marjoram, salt and pepper to taste, and 2½ cups of the giblet stock in a large bowl. Wipe the turkey inside and out with a damp cloth. Stuff the cavity with the dressing; truss and place on a rack in a roasting pan. Cut a piece of cheesecloth large enough to fit over the turkey. Soak the cloth in the melted butter and place over the turkey. Make an aluminum-foil tent over the turkey; press the

edges tightly to the rim of the roasting pan and place in oven for 20 minutes. Reduce heat to 350° F. and continue to roast until legs move freely and juices run yellow when thigh is pricked with a fork, about 5 hours or 15 minutes per pound. One hour before turkey is done, remove foil and cheese-cloth and baste with pan juices so turkey will brown. Let stand 10 minutes before serving.

To make the gravy, melt 2 teaspoons of the remaining butter in a large skillet over medium heat. Add the turkey liver and sauté 2 minutes each side. Cool. Finely chop the liver and set aside. Finely chop the reserved giblets and 1 quarter-section of the reserved carrot; set aside. Melt the remaining butter in the same skillet over medium-low heat. Whisk in the flour. Cook, stirring constantly, for 2 minutes. Whisk in 2 cups of the remaining giblet stock and simmer for 5 minutes. Stir in the chopped liver, chopped giblets, chopped carrot, remaining marjoram, and salt and pepper to taste; simmer 2 minutes longer.

Place turkey on a large platter. Garnish with fresh parsley. Pass gravy on the side.

Serves 8, with enough leftovers for another meal.

ABOVE: *The kitchen is roomy enough for two or more to make preparations for a big feast. The stained-glass windows above the glass doors were sold at auction at the Sea-mens Church Institute in New York. The sliding doors open onto a very small balcony (just big enough for two) that overlooks the horse pasture.*

FAR LEFT: *Ruth roasted the turkey right on a Wilton Armetale well-and-tree platter. Just before serving, we added the pumpkins and potatoes to the platter and placed it on a food warmer we salvaged from The Bird and Bottle. The whole meal was served from two serving pieces that kept warm all afternoon.*

A Family Thanksgiving

ABOVE: *Everything in place, we are assured of a long, leisurely meal.*

Steamed Vegetable Trio with Onion-Chestnut Sauce

Here's a hot vegetable bowl that gives freedom of choice to those at the table who have different ''favorite'' vegetables. It looks spectacular, too! Use a double steamer if you have one. Another surprise for us—we used a beautiful purple cauliflower, thinking it would look wonderful on the table. When we steamed it, however, it turned green. It still looked wonderful, but beware!

 3 tablespoons unsalted butter
 1 cup pearl onions, peeled
1½ cups whole dry-roasted chestnuts, plus extra for garnish
 2 tablespoons all-purpose flour
 1 cup giblet stock (see turkey recipe, page 38)
 1 cup half-and-half or light cream
  Salt and freshly ground black pepper
 4 turnips, trimmed
 1 head cauliflower, trimmed
 6 cups (2 10-ounce packages fresh) Brussels sprouts, washed and trimmed, with an *X* cut into each stem end

Melt 1 tablespoon of the butter in a large skillet over medium heat. Add the onions and sauté until golden brown, about 3 minutes. Remove with a slotted spoon and set aside. Add chestnuts to same skillet and sauté until browned (about 3 to 5 minutes).

Fall

Melt remaining butter in the top of a double boiler over simmering water. Whisk in flour and cook, stirring constantly, for 2 minutes. Whisk in stock and half-and-half. Continue to cook, stirring frequently, until sauce thickens. Stir in onions, chestnuts, and salt and pepper to taste. Remove from heat and keep warm.

Place turnips in the bottom tier of a double steamer filled with water. Place cauliflower in the top tier. Heat water to boiling, cover, and steam 12 minutes. Remove cauliflower and keep warm. Place Brussels sprouts in top tier, cover, and continue steaming for 8 minutes. (If you are steaming vegetables one at a time, steam the turnips 20 minutes, the cauliflower 12 minutes, and the Brussels sprouts 8 minutes.) Remove from heat and slice turnips into thin rounds. Line the inside of a large heated serving bowl with the turnip slices. Place the cauliflower in the center of bowl. Add the Brussels sprouts to the onion-chestnut sauce; toss until sprouts are well coated. Using a slotted spoon, add the sprouts to the serving bowl, making a ring around the cauliflower. Pour extra sauce in the center of the cauliflower and over the Brussels sprouts. Garnish with extra chestnuts and parsley. Serve immediately.

Serves 8–10.

Pumpkin Boxes

Steam a few extra mini-pumpkins, cut the tops off, and scrape out the seeds and strings. But instead of stuffing them, just allow them to dry. They hold their pumpkin shape marvelously and can be used as gift containers. Add dried flowers, potpourri, sweets, dried herbs—anything you like.

Stuffed Mini-Pumpkins

   8 mini-pumpkins (as uniform in size as possible)
   5 ripe McIntosh apples
   ½ cup chopped dates
2½ tablespoons sliced almonds, toasted
   4 teaspoons molasses

Preheat the oven to 350° F. Lightly butter a baking sheet or dish and set aside. Place the pumpkins in the bottom tier of a double steamer filled with water. Place apples on top tier. Heat water to boiling, cover, and steam 10 minutes. Remove apples, cover, and continue steaming 5 minutes longer. (If you are steaming the apples and pumpkins one at a time, steam the apples 10 minutes and the pumpkins 15.) Remove pumpkins and allow to cool slightly. Cut off tops of pumpkins and set aside. Scrape out seeds and strings. Set each pumpkin on the prepared baking sheet.

Peel, core, and slice the apples. Combine the apples, dates, almonds, and molasses in a bowl; toss until well mixed. Fill each pumpkin with the apple mixture. Replace tops on pumpkins and bake until completely warmed through, about 20 minutes.

Serves 8.

BELOW: *The entrance to the 1836 Barn is dressed up for Thanksgiving.*

Baked Sweet Potatoes

Our convection oven bakes these to a golden crispness that the conventional oven just can't achieve. If you have a convection oven, use it here.

  8 sweet potatoes, cut in half lengthwise
  2 tablespoons (¼ stick) unsalted butter, melted
      Salt and freshly ground black pepper

Preheat the oven to 350° F. Brush each potato with butter. Sprinkle with salt and pepper and place on a baking sheet. Bake until tender and the surfaces are crispy, about 1 hour.

     Serves 8.

Bert Greene's Apple Pie

Our late friend Bert Greene would have been a welcome guest at our table any Thanksgiving. We miss him terribly. It was his enthusiasm for The Silo and for our farm that encouraged us to photograph and write about our lives here. We were delighted and surprised to discover that his greatest love was honest country food served simply. He loved coming to teach at The Silo and staying here as our guest. We consider it the highest compliment that he found our way of living satisfying to his spirit as well as to his palate. So, here is his apple pie. It helps us remember his warmth, goodness, and generosity.

    1 recipe orange pastry crust (see recipe, page 43)
7–8 tart apples, peeled, cored, and cut into ½-inch slices
    2 ounces (⅓ cup plus 1½ tablespoons) all-purpose flour
    5 ounces (¾ cup) granulated sugar
   ¾ teaspoon ground cinnamon
   ⅛ teaspoon freshly grated nutmeg
   ½ teaspoon grated orange peel
   ½ teaspoon vanilla extract
   ½ cup honey
 2½ ounces (⅓ cup) dark brown sugar, lightly packed
      Pinch of ground ginger
 3½ tablespoons unsalted butter, chilled
    1 large egg, beaten
      Vanilla ice cream

Make the orange pastry crust and set aside. Place apples in a large bowl and toss with 1½ tablespoons flour. Add the granulated sugar, ½ teaspoon of the cinnamon, and the nutmeg, orange peel, and vanilla. Mix well. Stir in honey and let stand 1 hour.

Preheat the oven to 450° F. Combine remaining ⅓ cup flour, the remaining ¼ teaspoon cinnamon, the brown sugar, and the ginger in a small bowl. With 2 knives or a pastry blender, cut in 2 tablespoons butter until mixture resembles coarse crumbs.

On a lightly floured surface, roll out half the orange pastry crust dough to a ⅛-inch thickness and place in the bottom of a 9-inch pie plate. Trim the edges.

Drain the apple slices, reserving liquid. Set ¼ cup of the crumb mixture aside. Place a layer of apples in the pastry shell, add a layer of the crumb mixture, follow with another layer of apples, and repeat until all apples and crumbs are used. Use crumbs like mortar to build up the fruit. Dot apples with remaining 1½ tablespoons butter and sprinkle with 5 tablespoons reserved apple liquid and reserved crumb mixture.

Roll out the remaining dough and place over top of pie. Trim and flute the edges. Make vents in the top crust with a sharp knife and brush with beaten egg.

Bake on a foil-lined baking sheet for 5 minutes. Reduce heat to 350° F. and bake until golden, about 50 minutes longer. Serve with vanilla ice cream.

Serves 8–10.

Orange Pastry Crust

    12½ ounces (2½ cups) all-purpose flour
     ½ teaspoon salt
     8 tablespoons (1 stick) unsalted butter, chilled
     ½ cup solid vegetable shortening, chilled
     1 teaspoon grated orange peel
     ¼ cup cold orange juice

Sift the flour with salt into a large bowl. With 2 knives or a pastry blender, cut in butter and shortening until mixture is the texture of coarse crumbs. Add orange peel and mix.

Using a fork or knife, blend orange juice into flour mixture to form a soft dough. Do not overwork. Form into a ball, wrap in wax paper, and chill 1 hour.

Makes enough for one 9-inch double-crust pie.

TOP: *A set of English crocks holds kitchen staples.* ABOVE: *We love the look of copper pots and molds— they bring warmth, color, and comfort to the kitchen. But we also have learned to live with copper that is less than perfectly polished. Who has time to clean it all?*

A Family Thanksgiving

Pumpkin Pie

1 recipe short pastry crust (see recipe below)
1 16-ounce can pumpkin
1 cup honey
2 tablespoons molasses
2 teaspoons ground cinnamon
¼ teaspoon ground allspice
¼ teaspoon ground cloves
   Pinch of salt
4 large eggs
1 cup heavy cream
½ cup fresh cranberries, cooked

Roll the crust dough on a lightly floured surface to a ⅛-inch thickness and place it in the bottom of a 10-inch pie pan. Trim and flute the edges.

Preheat the oven to 450° F. Combine the pumpkin, honey, molasses, and spices in a food processor and process until well blended. With the processor on, add eggs one at a time, processing a few seconds after each addition. Transfer to a large bowl.

Beat the cream in a large bowl until doubled in volume. Fold into the pumpkin mixture. Pour into prepared pie shell and bake 10 minutes. Reduce heat to 350° F. and bake until a toothpick inserted in the center comes out clean, about 40 minutes longer. Cool. Arrange cranberries in a circle on top of pie.

Serves 8.

Short Pastry Crust

5 ounces (1 cup) all-purpose flour
   Pinch of salt
4 tablespoons (½ stick) unsalted butter, chilled and cut into
   bits
1½ tablespoons solid vegetable shortening, chilled
2–3 tablespoons cold water

Sift the flour and salt together into a large bowl. With 2 knives or a pastry blender, cut in the butter and shortening until mixture is the texture of coarse crumbs. Add only enough water to make a soft dough. Form into a ball, wrap in wax paper, and chill for at least 1 hour.

Makes enough for one 10-inch single-crust pie.

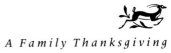

Winter

O n Hunt Hill Farm we've had some glorious winters,
with the silos and stone walls covered with snow.

WINTER

It's amazing that it can build up that high. In 1969, there was so much snow that it reached the windowsills on the first floor of the main house. A neighbor came by, walking on the stone wall—no road could be seen—and asked, "What do you need from the store?" Milk and cigarettes was the answer then. Our pantry was always filled; we could survive for quite a while.

Nothing is untouched by the snow. The farm becomes virgin territory and we take the first steps. Finally there is a narrow path all the way up the mountain—blue sky, sun, the snow *knirscht* underfoot. No one breathes too deeply—too cold. The dogs march in one line until suddenly there is a place where the snow is not so deep and off they go making their own tracks, white flying behind them.

At the cooking shed, there is winter life, too. We save branches from the old apple trees, make a fire, and throw a steak on the grill. We wrap potatoes in foil and throw them right in the fire. A pot of horseradish and a peppermill are all the seasonings we need. Beer and wine chill in the snow and, while we cut into the steak, apples sizzle on the grill. There is nothing like that smell and sound.

Then come the dark and cold wintry days. All fires are burning in the stoves; the little Upland that heats the downstairs, the Garrison in the kitchen, and the big Fisher in The Silo Gallery. We love the smell of wood burning all day long.

In the evening, we build the fire in the Great Room fireplace. Skitch lights all the candles—a favorite moment of winter.

By early December, we put the tree up and collect the presents around it. Then it's time for making lists and baking those gifts of cookies and breads. *Am Heiligen Abend*—December 24, 6:00 P.M.—we celebrate. A good meal, Skitch plays the organ, and the children and grandchildren open their presents. What joy!

PRECEDING PAGES: *We planted our lower pastures with 5,000 Christmas trees. Our volunteer fire department cares for the trees, and will cut and sell them to benefit the volunteer corps. Replanting and harvesting will go on each year thereafter.* ABOVE: *One pasture at the farm remains completely wild—a refuge for birds, who eat the berries and nest in the thick brush.*

TOP: *The large wheel of the steam engine is caught by the first snow.*

ABOVE: *Apples roast over a wood fire—this is simple pleasure for all the senses. We enjoy the smoke, the sizzle, the smell as the apples puff and hiss and, finally, the taste, as we eat them as hot as we can stand.*

RIGHT: *The Silo as seen from Mrs. Anderson's field. This is the kind of day we cherish—a blanket of snow, a radiant sky, and air so cold we can hardly breathe.*

*Presents from
the Kitchen*

•

Winter
Eintopfgerichte

•

Sauerbraten for Six

•

*Dinner for Four
in the Silo*

•

Henderson Breakfasts

LEFT: *Skitch is a member of the
Connecticut Antique Machinery Soci-
ety, a group of steam-engine enthusi-
asts. When he's finished restoring this
engine, he's promised it to the soci-
ety's museum.* ABOVE: *The 1951
Chevy truck has lived on this road all
its life. It was originally owned by
Kathleen and Howard Pitchard, who
sold it to Ruth so she could give it to
Skitch for his birthday.*

Presents from the Kitchen

There's nothing more pleasing than a homemade gift with a personal touch. These holiday presents are made from simple sculpted bread and cookie doughs, and they've never failed to delight whoever receives them.

Basic recipes and directions are provided, but your playfulness and individual expression are what will make these presents memorable. Attach a favorite ornament or make a bow from old material—Ruth never throws away old denim or anything cotton and colorful; she even saved the extra wallpaper from our children's rooms for all these years. Every so often, she will wrap a small present for one of them with it. Or, pipe a name or a date on the dough in icing. The smallest thing can make the biggest difference.

Basic Bread Sculpture Dough

○

Holiday Bubble Wreath

○

Angel

○

Santa

FAR LEFT: *A 25-foot tree dominates The Silo Gallery every year; people drive for miles to see it. This one is trimmed with apples, cinnamon sticks, wooden beads, and soft sculptures by Mary Ann Sabados. The cow is by Woody Jackson.*
LEFT: *From the driveway just outside The Silo barnyard, we can look across Crossmon Road to the 1836 Barn.* ABOVE: *The engine is dressed for the holidays.*

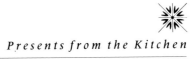

Divide dough into the portions required for your design, saving a small piece of dough for decorative detail. Have lightly greased baking sheets lined with foil or parchment paper ready and shape your sculptures right on them.

For large sculptures, overlap two rimless baking sheets and adjust them to fit your oven, allowing at least one inch all around the sheets for even heat circulation, and cover these with foil. For large solid areas, or as a base, first shape the dough into a ball and roll it out or pat it into the desired form.

If you are creating your own design, use simple shapes—small details become distorted upon baking. Do not make dough thicker than an inch, since it may crack when baked. To create texture (such as in the angel's wings), snip dough with the tips of a pair of scissors. Attach dough pieces with the egg wash described in the basic recipe.

Leftover dough, molded and baked with the sculptures, makes delicious dinner rolls.

Basic Bread Sculpture Dough

1 ¼-ounce package active dry yeast
3 tablespoons warm water (105°–115° F.)
4 ounces (½ cup plus 4 teaspoons) granulated
    sugar
¾ cup milk
8 tablespoons (1 stick) unsalted butter, cut into bits
1½–2 pounds (5–6⅓ cups) all-purpose flour
¾ teaspoon salt
1 teaspoon ground cinnamon
4 large eggs, at room temperature
1 large egg yolk
1 tablespoon water

Dissolve the yeast in warm water with 1 teaspoon of the sugar in a small bowl. Let stand 10 minutes.

Meanwhile, scald the milk; remove from heat and stir in the butter. Allow to cool.

Combine 5 ounces (1½ cup) of the flour with the salt, cinnamon, and remaining sugar in a large bowl. Make a well in the center and add the yeast mixture. Add eggs one at a time, beating well after each addition. Gradually stir in enough of the remaining flour to form a soft dough. Turn out on a lightly floured surface and knead until smooth and elastic, about 15 minutes. Place dough in a lightly greased bowl, cover with a towel, and let rise in a warm place until doubled in volume, about 1½ hours.

Punch dough down and divide in half. Shape each half as desired and set aside until puffy, about 20 minutes.

Preheat the oven to 375° F. Beat the egg yolk with the water in a small bowl. Place bread shapes on a lightly greased baking sheet. Brush shapes with egg wash and bake until golden and bread sounds hollow when tapped gently on the bottom, about 30 minutes.

Makes enough dough for 2 sculptures.

Holiday Bubble Wreath

We love wreaths because the round shape is comforting and reassuring. You can eat this one right away or you can preserve it with clear lacquer spray and hang it or use it as a centerpiece. Here is where a bow made of material from some time remembered is a wonderful gesture.

Place an inverted ovenproof custard cup in the center of a prepared baking sheet. After punching down half the basic sculpture dough, divide it into 33 equal pieces. Form 32 balls of dough. Arrange dough balls in a circle around the custard cup in 2 layers.

Roll out the remaining piece of dough. Either cut out a bow shape with a sharp knife or form a bow using your fingers. Place bow on wreath. Set wreath aside in a warm place to rise for 20 minutes.

Bake according to directions on page 54. Five minutes before wreath is finished baking, carefully remove the custard cup.

Makes 1 wreath.

Angel

This angel will want to take on its own personality. Let it. Once, for someone we know who loves dried flowers, this angel held a bouquet of dried roses.

After punching down half the basic dough, divide it into 2 parts, one part double the size of the other. Place the larger piece on a lightly floured surface; press or roll it into a triangle and place it on the prepared baking sheet. Divide the remaining dough into 4 parts (the fourth part need only be half the size of the other three). Form one of the larger pieces into a ball. Roll flat and press it onto the top of the triangle to form the angel's head. Roll out the 2 remaining large pieces to form triangular shapes. Press the narrow end of the shapes into the large triangle to form the angel's arms or wings.

Roll out the fourth portion of dough into a long thin strip. Break strips and bits off and attach, using egg wash, to form angel's hair, features, trim, etc. Set aside in a warm place to rise for 20 minutes.

Bake according to directions on page 54.

Makes 1 angel.

TOP AND ABOVE: *A good basic dough lets anyone be a sculptor.*

FAR LEFT: *The hearth in the Great Room of the 1836 Barn is decked with needlepoint stockings, a soft-sculpture Santa, and a toy from Skitch's collection.*

Santa

Add a sack made from a piece of burlap and put a small present in it.

After punching down half the basic dough, divide it in half. Roll out one portion on a lightly floured surface into a square shape and place it on the prepared baking sheet. Divide the remaining dough into 2 portions, one portion double the size of the other. Divide the larger portion in half. Press one half into a circle to form Santa's head.

Divide the other half into equal parts. Use one part to form Santa's arms and the other part to form Santa's belt. Use remaining dough to form Santa's hat, buttons, nose, beard, legs, etc. Set aside in a warm place to rise for 20 minutes.

Bake according to directions on page 54.

Makes 1 Santa.

ABOVE: *From a collection of Skitch's, a medieval carving of a Bürgermeister hangs in the Great Room. Below, Ruth's treasury of pewter boxes and molds sits on an antique spool chest that stores flatware.*

RIGHT: *Give a cookie in a hand-carved bowl as a present. When the cookie is gone, the bowl lives on!*

FAR RIGHT: *The skylight above the stairwell directs light onto the truck parked on the landing. Above it is a Spanish ox-yoke shelf, where Hans's geodes still rest.*

The Gingerbread Family

Every season offers opportunities to make and give away cookies. But this cookie family makes a very special Christmas present, either to a single cookie lover or to a whole family. This family is made from our basic gingerbread turkey place-card cookie recipe (page 36), but you can also use the shortbread horse cookie recipe (page 26). Pipe the icing to create the characters any way you like. Adding a name, too, can give the cookie extra personality.

What the family travels in is also a present. Choose an unusual basket, antique box, or tin. You will be amazed at how gratified your friends will be with this simple gift.

Winter Eintopfgerichte

Among Germans, a whole meal prepared in one pot is called an *Eintopfgericht*. Each state in Germany has its own unique and traditional rendition and every regional cookbook claims to publish the "original" *Eintopf*.

Ruth loves creating and serving her own *Eintopf* in wintertime because, like a New England boiled dinner, an Irish stew, or a pot au feu, an *Eintopf* is the perfect cold-weather meal. The house fills with warm cooking smells. Your guests come in from the cold to the comfort of rich aromas—what an appetite whetter! They sit down to a hearty dinner served informally in one bowl. If more than the invited number show up, as often happens here on the farm, the meal stretches and stretches to feed the extra guests. Besides, making an *Eintopf* appeals to the imagination. There are no rules about which ingredients must cook together or which flavors should mingle. It's a simple, hearty, satisfying meal that takes care of body and soul.

Yellow Chicken *Eintopf*

◦

Red Pig *Eintopf*

◦

Purple Pork Roast
Schlemmertopf

◦

Gaisburger Marsch

LEFT: *This is the entry to Hunt Hill Cottage, where our friend June Freemanzon lives when she comes from the city for weekends. When she gathers us together for food and visiting, the smallest house seems to hold the most life and laughter. The old English coatrack holds Ruth's parents' walking sticks and hats.*
BELOW: *On the winter pond, Mia and Ryan are the first out on skates.*

Yellow Chicken *Eintopf*

For years, people have associated beans and dried peas with bad times, lean times, hard times. We're so glad the day of the bean is back. The yellow split peas give this Eintopf *a hearty taste but the look is delicate, almost ethereal.*

- 4 pounds dried yellow split peas
- 2 4½-pound chickens
- 6 quarts water
- 2 large cloves garlic (we use elephant garlic), peeled and bruised
- 8 white peppercorns
- 4 stalks celery (with leaves), quartered
- 2 medium parsnips
- 2 medium carrots
- 2 medium onions, peeled
- 2 teaspoons salt
- 4 bay leaves
- 2 large heads cauliflower, separated into medium florets

ABOVE: *Dinner is informally served in one of the cozy corners of the kitchen. The soft sculptures of women in aprons are by Constance Harper.*

RIGHT: *Another prize from Ruth's tureen collection, this rooster keeps the* Eintopf *warm for a long time. Using lemon halves and reamer, each guest seasons his plate with juice to taste.*

OPPOSITE, TOP: *In another corner of the kitchen, a low pine table is set for the Red Pig* Eintopf. *On the wall is a rare watercolor-and-pencil sketch by Stanford White. The lamp is made from the (now defunct) copper fire extinguisher.*

OPPOSITE, BOTTOM: *Ruth brought these durable white soup plates from Germany when she first moved to the United States.*

2 cups croutons
1 lemon, sliced
Chopped fresh dill

Soak the peas in a large pot of water at least overnight. Drain and set aside. Place the chickens, including innards (but not the liver) in a large pot. Cover with the water and add the next 8 ingredients. Heat to boiling, reduce heat, and simmer for 1 hour. Transfer chickens to a platter. Allow broth to cool, then skim fat and strain.

Return broth to the same large pot. Add the peas and heat to boiling; reduce heat and simmer until tender, about 2 hours. Fifteen minutes before peas are done, add the cauliflower and return to a simmer.

Meanwhile, cut the chickens into parts with kitchen scissors. Five minutes before peas are done, add the chicken parts. Continue to simmer until chicken is warmed through, about 5 minutes more.

Serve with croutons, sliced lemon, and dill.

Serves 12–14.

Red Pig *Eintopf*

Men love this Eintopf! *It's probably the deep color and the blend of smoked flavors that appeal to their appetites. We used smoked sausages, which were pre-cooked, and just browned them. If you wish to use other sausages, suit your own taste, but be sure to brown them.*

  4 pounds dried red beans, soaked overnight
  6 quarts ham stock (see recipe, page 62)
16 Virginia smoked sausages
  2 pounds pre-cooked Smithfield ham, cut into 2-inch pieces
    Red pig pumpernickel breadsticks (see recipe, page 62)
  1 large onion, finely chopped

Drain the beans and place in a large soup pot. Add the ham stock and heat to boiling; reduce heat and simmer gently over low heat until beans are tender, about 2½ hours. Prick the sausages with a pin. Heat a lightly oiled heavy skillet over medium heat. Add the sausages and brown on all sides. Set aside. A half-hour before serving, add the ham and sausages to the beans. To serve, ladle into individual soup bowls and top each with 3 or 4 breadsticks. Serve the chopped onions on the side.

Serves 12.

TOP: *Framed by the skylight, the Armetale and Swiss copper pots seem to glow.* ABOVE: *Old English baby's feeding bowls feature the alphabet and nursery rhymes.*

Ham Stock

The secret to this stock is to use a ham bone with some meat still on it.

- 1 ham bone, about 1½ pounds
- 8 quarts water
- 2 parsnips
- 2 carrots
- 4 bay leaves
- 2 black peppercorns
- 4 stalks celery
- 5 whole cloves

Combine all ingredients in a large soup pot. Heat to boiling, reduce heat, and simmer until liquid is reduced to 6 quarts. Strain.

Makes 6 quarts.

Red Pig Pumpernickel Breadsticks

These belong on the priority list in the ''little things mean a lot'' department. Second only to our love affair with cookies is our passion for breadsticks and croutons. Because the secret to a good Eintopf is to be able to eat it all in one bowl, we don't want guests to have to handle or butter bread or rolls. These breadsticks add texture and flavor to the meal with no extra effort from hungry guests. And the next day and the day after that, they make terrific additions to other meals, or you can dip them in sour cream or yogurt and red pepper jelly and serve as a snack.

- 12 slices pumpernickel bread
- 6 tablespoons (¾ stick) unsalted butter
- Salt and pepper

Cut the bread into thin strips, about 1½ inches wide. Melt 2 tablespoons of the butter in a large skillet over medium heat. Add several strips of the bread and sauté until crisp, then drain on paper towels and sprinkle with salt and pepper to taste. Repeat the process until all strips are sautéed.

Makes 48 breadsticks.

Purple Pork Roast *Schlemmertopf*

All cooking in clay is an Eintopfgericht, *whether you use a* Schlemmertopf *or other clay baker. And, prepared this way, one-pot meals can be both foolproof and gratifying. Skitch, when cooking for himself, will throw a few ingredients in the* Schlemmertopf, *put it in the oven, and enjoy a meal two hours later. What's wonderful about cooking in clay is that no extra fats or oils are used; the meats and vegetables cook in their own juices. The flavor is out of this world. Give clay cookers as gifts to young cooks; it's hard to go wrong with any meal prepared this way. And, of course, there's only one pot to clean!*

Note About Clay Cookers

Never use soap to clean your clay pots, unless, like the bottom of the *Schlemmertopf,* it has a glaze. If your pot *does* have a glaze, then you can use a mild detergent. If it is an unglazed pot, scrub it with hot water only. If it needs a better cleaning, soak it in water and baking soda, then brush it out with a strong bristle brush. And don't worry about inevitable spots and discoloration; that's what gives your pot a country, lived-with look. Also, in the event of breakage, take heart; we've been known to use two tops after having lost both bottoms along the way.

>   3 red apples, cored and sliced
>   Juice of 2 lemons
>   12 prunes
>   1 3½-pound center-cut pork roast, with bone*
>   Salt and freshly ground black pepper
>   4 ounces prepared honey mustard
>   1 head red cabbage, about 2½ pounds, shredded
>   2 tablespoons light brown sugar
>   2 tablespoons balsamic or red-wine vinegar
>   1 teaspoon dried marjoram
>   6 baking potatoes
>   1 onion, studded with 30 cloves

Sprinkle the apples with half the lemon juice and set aside.

Place the prunes in a medium bowl, cover with water, and allow to soak 30 minutes.

Wash and dry the meat thoroughly. Sprinkle with remaining lemon juice, salt, and pepper. Spread the honey mustard over the outside of the roast and in between the chops. Set aside.

Combine the cabbage, apples, brown sugar, vinegar, and marjoram in the *Schlemmertopf;* toss well. Place pork on top of bed of cabbage. Arrange the potatoes, onion, and prunes around the pork. Cover and place in a cold oven. Set the thermostat to 425° F. and roast for 2 hours.

Remove pot from oven and place on a wooden board or thick towel. Serve directly from the *Schlemmertopf* or unmold contents onto a platter.

Serves 6.

*Ask your butcher to cut through the bone to create 6 chops loosely attached to the bone.

Gaisburger Marsch

ABOVE: *Ruth needs her largest Calphalon pot to prepare this* Eintopf. *We often leave it on the stove for friends to serve themselves.*

This traditional Eintopf *from Württemberg is named after an historical local conflict in which—according to folklore—all the men from Gaisburg were taken prisoner. Their wives were allowed to bring the men their meals. However, the women were permitted only one bowl or pot for each man. Each* Frau *packed her one pot with nourishing ingredients—meat, broth, bones with marrow, vegetables,* Spätzle—*and delivered the* Eintopf *piping hot. The men stayed well fed until the conflict was settled. Today, many of Germany's decorated chefs include the* Gaisburger Marsch *on their menus.*

4 tablespoons (½ stick) butter
1 6-pound beef shank, boned (about 4 pounds meat)*
1 beef shank bone, about 2 pounds*
2 onions, sliced
2 teaspoons dried marjoram
  Salt and freshly ground black pepper
6 quarts water
2 carrots, halved and quartered
1 parsnip, halved and quartered
2 cloves garlic, peeled and bruised
1 whole onion, peeled
4 bay leaves
4 stalks celery, quartered
  Spätzle (see recipe, page 65)

Melt the butter in a large soup pot. Add the meat and brown on all sides. Remove meat with a slotted spoon and set aside. Add bones and sear until browned, then remove with a slotted spoon and set aside. Add the sliced onions and cook until golden brown, about 8 minutes. Add the marjoram and salt and pepper to taste.

Return meat to the soup pot. Add the water, carrots, parsnip, garlic, whole onion, bay leaves, and celery. Heat to boiling, reduce heat, and simmer, covered, for 1 hour. Add the bones and simmer 1 hour more.

Using a slotted spoon, transfer meat, bones, and vegetables to a plate. Allow broth to cool, then skim the fat.

Meanwhile, cut the meat into 2-inch pieces. Heat the broth to boiling and add the meat and vegetables. Reduce heat and simmer until meat is warmed through, about 5 minutes. Just before serving, add a generous portion of *Spätzle*.

Serves 16.

*Ask your butcher to bone the meat and to cut both bones into 2½-inch lengths.

Spätzle

In Schwabenländle, cooks are renowned for their Spätzle making. They spread the dough on a hand-held wooden board and, with unmatched deftness, rapidly cut the dough into tiny pieces that fall into boiling water. Most people, however, need a colander or a Spätzle maker.

    2½ cups all-purpose flour
    1⅛ teaspoons salt
    ⅛ teaspoon ground white pepper
    ⅛ teaspoon freshly grated nutmeg
    3 large eggs
    1 cup milk
    2 quarts water
    1 tablespoon vegetable oil

Sift the flour, ⅛ teaspoon salt, and spices together into a large bowl. Make a well in the center. Beat the eggs and milk in a small bowl and pour this mixture into the well of the dry mixture. Stir until a soft dough forms.

    Combine the water, oil, and remaining salt in a large saucepan. Heat to boiling. Place about one-third of the dough in a lightly oiled colander or *Spätzle* maker and hold it over the boiling water. Using a wooden spoon, gently push dough through the holes into the boiling water. Cook *Spätzle* until the water returns to a boil and the *Spätzle* rise to the surface, about 1 minute. Remove with a slotted spoon. Repeat the process until all dough is cooked. Add to *Gaisburger Marsch* and serve immediately.

Serves 16 when added to the *Gaisburger Marsch*.

ABOVE: *As seen from Hunt Hill Cottage, one of the large maples and the roof of The Silo garage are framed by the window and painted with winter sunlight.*

BELOW: *In Hunt Hill Cottage, a sewing-machine stand with a wooden top makes a buffet table for the Gaisburger Marsch.*

Sauerbraten for Six

A dark February night is ideal for candlelight, a few friends, and sauerbraten. This favorite meal in our family can't be improvised at the last minute. You need at least four days to marinate the meat. However, putting it together is simple. Our dinner guests make themselves comfortable right in the kitchen while we take care of the final touches. Our kitchen is truly the heart of the home. A lot of living takes place there—and certainly a lot of eating. A dining table seats six, two cozy corners seat four each, and six old English pub stools attend the counter.

Sauerbraten

∘

Lightly Steamed Parsnips, Carrots, and Peas

∘

Serviettenkloss

∘

Plumped Fruit with Applejack Cream

LEFT: *In January, Ruth starts the paperwhites in bowls. By the dark days of February, they bloom and fill the house with the promise of spring. Here, they surround the room where the family-style meal is set. Candles are vital at the Henderson table—Ruth lights one even when she eats alone.* ABOVE: *Over the entrance to the 1836 Barn is the window of the Great Room. The stone silo in shadow stores firewood.*

ABOVE: *We prefer to serve as much of the meal as we can on one platter. For this dinner, the vegetables add terrific color.*

Sauerbraten

You don't need a first-rate cut of meat for this recipe because of the length of time it takes to marinate. You also don't need such a large piece of beef. Remember that we plan for other meals from this one.

  1 10- to 12-pound boneless shoulder or rump roast
      Salt and freshly ground black pepper
  9 cups water
  3 cups balsamic or red-wine vinegar
10 whole cloves
  2 cloves garlic
  1 large onion, sliced
  1 cup dark brown sugar, loosely packed
  6 black peppercorns
  5 bay leaves
  8 tablespoons (1 stick) unsalted butter
  2 medium carrots
  2 medium stalks celery
  2 medium onions, peeled and cut in half
  6 cups warm water or beef broth
24 honey cookies or ginger snaps

Rub the meat with salt and pepper and place in a Dutch oven. Set aside.

Combine the next 7 ingredients and 3 bay leaves in a large saucepan. Heat to boiling, reduce heat, and simmer 10 minutes. Allow to cool slightly. Pour marinade over meat. Cover and refrigerate 4 days, turning every 24 hours. Remove meat from marinade and pat dry. Allow the meat to return to room temperature and reserve marinade.

Melt the butter in a heavy pot over medium heat. Add the carrots, celery, and medium onions and brown. Transfer to a plate and add the meat to the pot; brown meat on all sides. Add the 6 cups water, carrots, celery, onions, 2 remaining bay leaves, and 1 cup of the marinade. Heat to boiling, then reduce to a low simmer. Cover and cook 1 hour. Turn beef over. Crumble cookies and add to the pot, then cover and simmer 1½ hours longer. Meat should be well done but firm to the touch of a knife.

To make the gravy, remove meat from pot and let stand. Pass liquid and vegetables through a food mill; return to the pot. Taste the gravy. Whisk in a small amount of reserved marinade if needed, and continue to simmer until warmed through.

To serve, slice the beef and place on a heated serving platter with the steamed vegetables (see page 69). Serve the gravy on the side.

Serves 6, with enough leftovers for another meal.

Next-Day Hot Sauerbraten Sandwich

Slice the sauerbraten and place it on a slice of dark bread. Cover with hot gravy.

Or, purée the leftover vegetables, season them any way you desire, and use as a spread for your sauerbraten sandwich—much better than butter.

Or, slice the vegetables and layer them with the meat between slices of bread.

Lightly Steamed Parsnips, Carrots, and Peas

Light steaming so enhances the flavor of these vegetables that we don't need to use any spices. We prefer to let the gravy from the sauerbraten give them any additional flavor they may need.

- 6 parsnips, peeled and cut in half lengthwise
- 6 carrots, peeled
- 1 10-ounce package frozen or fresh peas

Place parsnips and carrots in a steamer and fill the bottom with about 1 inch of water. Heat to boiling, cover, and steam 6 minutes. Add peas and steam 3 minutes longer. Arrange on platter with sauerbraten.

Serves 6.

Next-Day Vegetables

For a memorable side dish, we purée the vegetables in a blender or food processor, combine 1 cup of purée with ½ cup buttermilk in a saucepan, warm through over medium heat, and season with salt and pepper.

Puréed vegetables can also make a wonderful dip for breadsticks or a unique sandwich spread; just season 1 cup puréed vegetables with a little curry.

Serviettenkloss

This is another traditional German dish. Tasting somewhat like a savory bread pudding, it's a great substitute for potatoes. Serviettenkloss *adds a different character and comfort to the meal. We like it best served warm, but it's also wonderful cold.*

- 8 cups bread cubes
- ¼ cup evaporated milk
- 4 medium eggs, well beaten
- 2 tablespoons (¼ stick) unsalted butter
- 1 onion, finely chopped
- 3 tablespoons chopped fresh parsley
- ½ teaspoon freshly grated nutmeg
  Salt
- 3 scallions, trimmed

Combine the bread cubes, milk, and eggs in a large bowl. Set aside.

Melt the butter in a medium skillet over medium heat. Add the onion and cook until soft, about 5 minutes. Add onion to bread mixture and toss until well mixed. Add 2 tablespoons parsley and the nutmeg and mix well. Add salt to taste.

Fill a tall soup pot with water and heat to boiling. Reduce heat so that

ABOVE: *An underplate is a necessity for us because we always heat the dinner plates.*

ABOVE: *This is a sentimental collection: watches, lighters from the days when we all smoked, and a model of the Mercedes 300 SL that Skitch owned when he and Ruth courted.*

water boils gently. Form the bread mixture into a ball and place in the center of a linen or cotton towel or large cloth napkin. Tie 2 diagonal corners of the towel in a knot, loosely binding the bread mixture. Tie the remaining 2 diagonal corners in the same fashion. Now you should have what looks like a hobo's sack. Slide the handle of a long wooden spoon under the knots and place sack in the boiling water, allowing the sack to hang from the spoon and the spoon to rest its ends on the rim of the pot. Cover and boil gently 15 to 20 minutes. Remove to a platter, untie cloth, and unmold onto a serving dish. Garnish with whole fresh scallions and remaining chopped parsley. Slice and serve with sauerbraten and generous ladel of gravy.

Serves 8.

Plumped Fruit with Applejack Cream

Use any dried fruit you like for this. We like to soak ours in a tall, narrow crock so the fruit doesn't swim about. Use a minimum amount of water.

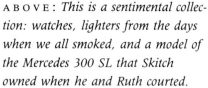

    2 11-ounce packages mixed dried fruit
    1 16-ounce container sour cream
    2 tablespoons light brown sugar
    1 tablespoon applejack or apple butter
    1 vanilla bean, cut into several bits

Place the fruit in a medium bowl and cover with water. Allow to stand several hours. Drain just before serving.

Combine the sour cream, brown sugar, applejack or apple butter, and vanilla bean in a bowl. Stir until well blended.

To serve, divide fruit among individual serving bowls. Add a generous dollop of applejack cream to each.

Serves 8.

RIGHT: *Plumped fruit, a simple pleasure and an easy dessert, is served from the hutch next to the kitchen table. The high chair is a treasure from Vermont. Pitchers are by Ted Keller.*

Dinner for Four in the Silo

Round rooms give us pleasure. There's a magical appeal left over from our love of fairy tales and castles. We are lucky to have four silos here on the farm. For dinner-in-the-round, we use the dining room in the wooden silo right off the kitchen. Dinner for four there is warm and cozy.

Round or rolled foods are also a favorite of ours. They're so versatile; you can serve them hot or cold, made fresh or the day before. Cold and sliced, they're terrific hors d'oeuvres; and they can be beautiful, depending on what you use as stuffing. Hot with gravy, they make an irresistible, homey meal.

We cooked for eight (except for dessert) and served four, knowing that the next day we would enjoy the repeat performance.

Spinach Chiffonade Beef Soup

o

Rouladen und Sosse

o

Schupfnudeln

o

Simple Carrots

o

Simple Peas

o

Pump-Raspberry Surprise

FAR LEFT: *The wooden silo at the 1836 Barn houses a hot tub on the ground floor and this game-dining room above. Baskets warm the walls and an antique roulette game is the centerpiece.* LEFT: *Our store was named for these silos. One, the ''glass silo,'' displays glassware. The other offers craft works for sale. The lantern on the path is from turn-of-the-century New York City.* ABOVE: *This is Skitch's favorite meal—* Rouladen, *vegetables, and* Schupfnudeln.

Spinach Chiffonade Beef Soup

Ask your butcher to cut the marrow bones for you and to cut the beef from the shank bone. It makes such a difference in this soup.

12 2-inch pieces beef bone with marrow
1½ pounds shin beef
¼ cup vegetable oil
2 leeks, rinsed well
2 onions
4 stalks celery
4 carrots
5 large sprigs parsley
4 bay leaves
4 quarts water
  Salt and pepper
8 large spinach leaves, washed, stems removed, and leaves
   patted dry
1 baguette, thinly sliced in rounds and toasted

Preheat the oven to 500° F. Place bones and meat on a rack in a roasting pan. Roast for 50 minutes. (There will be much sputtering and some smoking from your oven. Stay nearby.)

Heat the oil in a large soup pot. Add the leeks, onions, celery, and carrots; sauté until lightly browned. Add roasted bones and meat, parsley, bay leaves, and water. Heat to boiling, reduce heat, and simmer, uncovered, over low heat until liquid is reduced to 3 quarts, about 2 hours. Skim foam and fat as stock simmers. Strain and add salt and pepper to taste. Return to pot and keep warm over very low heat. Scoop the marrow from the bones with a spoon and place marrow in a small heatproof dish. Keep warm by placing dish in a hot-water bath in a small saucepan.

Arrange spinach in 2 stacks of 4 leaves each. Roll each stack lengthwise, so it looks like a cigar. Cut each stack crosswise into very thin strips, about ⅛ inch wide. Each strip will unroll to form 4 long ribbons of spinach.

To serve, ladle broth into individual soup bowls. Drop a generous portion of spinach ribbons lightly over broth. Serve with toasted baguette spread with warm marrow.

Serves 4.

FAR RIGHT: *Mary Ekstrom, who works at The Silo, taught Ruth how to make this soup. The delicious secret is a stock made from scratch. But it is terrific even if you must substitute canned broth.*

Rouladen und Sosse

This is Skitch's favorite meat dish. The beauty of it is that you can prepare it ahead of time. Also, serving lots of people becomes simple because each serving is self-contained. There's no slicing or spooning up portions.

8 thin slices top round of beef, about 7 ounces each
½ cup prepared mustard
8 strips lean bacon
4 dill pickles, quartered lengthwise
1 large onion, finely chopped
2½ teaspoons dried marjoram
8 tablespoons (1 stick) unsalted butter
4 large mushrooms, halved
2 medium carrots
1 medium onion, halved
6 tablespoons all-purpose flour
1 quart beef broth, heated
2 bay leaves

BELOW: *Ruth likes to serve these* Rouladen *right in the gravy, so they stay moist.*

Spread each piece of beef with 1 tablespoon mustard. Then, to each piece, add 1 strip bacon placed lengthwise, 2 spears of pickle placed crosswise,

and 1 teaspoon chopped onion. Sprinkle beef with marjoram. Roll up and secure with a skewer or kitchen twine tied in several places. Melt butter in a Dutch oven or 5-quart casserole over medium heat. Add the beef rolls 3 at a time and sauté until brown, about 2½ minutes per side. Be careful not to scorch! Transfer beef rolls to a plate.

Add the mushrooms, carrots, and halved onion to the pan; sauté over medium heat until vegetables are lightly browned. Gradually whisk in the flour; continue whisking until flour is lightly browned. Slowly whisk in broth. Add bay leaves. Heat to boiling, reduce heat, and add roulades; cover and simmer over low heat 1 hour.

Preheat the oven to 350° F. Transfer Rouladen to an ovenproof serving dish and remove the skewers or string. Strain the gravy or pass it through a food mill. Pour gravy over Rouladen, cover dish with foil, and heat in oven 30 minutes.

Serves 4, with enough left over for another meal.

Schupfnudeln

Here is another dish that takes time but is certainly worth the effort.

- 6 baked potatoes, cooled
- 2 large eggs, lightly beaten
- 1 cup all-purpose flour
- ½ teaspoon freshly ground nutmeg
- 1 teaspoon salt
- 3 tablespoons unsalted butter
- 1 tablespoon chopped fresh parsley

The day before serving, cut the potatoes in half lengthwise and scoop out the insides. Rice the potatoes or push them through a strainer and place them in a large bowl. Add the eggs, flour, nutmeg, and salt. Stir until a soft dough forms. Knead briefly on a lightly floured board, then break off a small piece and roll it into a 2-inch-long finger shape. Repeat the process until all the dough is rolled into finger shapes. Drop the fingers into a large pot of boiling salted water. When *Schupfnudeln* rise to the surface, remove them with a slotted spoon, drain, allow to cool, and refrigerate overnight.

Just before serving, melt 2 tablespoons of the butter in a large skillet. Add half the *Schupfnudeln* and sauté until golden. Transfer to an ovenproof dish and keep warm in a low oven. Melt remaining butter and sauté remaining *Schupfnudeln*. Serve garnished with parsley.

Serves 8.

ABOVE: Schupfnudeln *is a Swabian national dish. "Schupf" means push, and these are made by pushing potato dough into rolls. Ruth often prepares these the day before.*

Simple Carrots

    2 pounds carrots, trimmed, peeled, and cut into 1-inch pieces
    2 tablespoons (¼ stick) unsalted butter, cut into bits
    ⅛ teaspoon salt
    ⅛ teaspoon sugar

Arrange carrots in a single layer in a saucepan or large skillet. Add the butter and sprinkle with salt and sugar. Add just enough water to cover. Cut a circle of parchment paper the same circumference as the pot or skillet and place directly over the carrots. Cover the pot and bring to a boil; reduce heat and simmer gently until all the water has evaporated and carrots are tender, about 15 minutes.

Serve immediately.

Serves 4–6.

TOP: *We serve simple vegetables because the flavor of the meat and gravy should stand out at this meal.* ABOVE: *Leftovers are arranged in an ovenproof dish and stored. The next day's lunch warms up easily.*

Simple Peas

    2 pounds fresh green peas, shelled, or 2 10-ounce packages
        frozen peas
      Salt and freshly ground black pepper
    2 tablespoons unsalted butter, softened
      Pinch of sugar

Cook the peas in boiling water until just tender, about 3 to 4 minutes. Drain. Stir in butter until melted. Add sugar and salt and pepper to taste. Serve immediately.

Serves 8.

OPPOSITE, TOP: *In 1952, this silo held silage to feed Joann, whose nameplate remains in the 1836 Barn.* OPPOSITE, BOTTOM: *The dessert is a robust ending to the Rou-laden dinner. It is served on one of Ted Keller's cow plates.*

Pump-Raspberry Surprise

    ½ loaf fresh pumpernickel bread, thinly sliced
    4 ounces semisweet chocolate, shaved or grated
    ¼ cup light rum or cognac
    2 pints fresh raspberries, picked over
      Crème fraîche (see recipe, page 79), whipped

Cut the crust from the bread slices and finely crumble the slices into a large bowl. Add the chocolate and flavoring and stir until mixture is moist. Place a soft mound of the mixture in each of 4 dessert glasses, until each glass is about one-third full. Add raspberries to create another layer. Top generously with whipped crème fraîche.

Serves 4.

Crème Fraîche

    4 cups heavy cream
    3 tablespoons buttermilk

Combine the cream and buttermilk in a large bowl; mix well. Pour into a glass jar with a tight-fitting lid, cover, and let stand in a warm place until lightly thickened, about 20 hours. Refrigerate 24 hours.

    To serve whipped, lightly beat 1 cup of the cream mixture and top each serving with a generous dollop. Crème fraîche will keep 10 days in the refrigerator.

Makes 4 cups.

Henderson Breakfasts

*B*reakfasts are special for both of us, for different reasons. Ruth's mother liked to entertain at Sunday breakfast, and the Einsiedel *Frühstück* became known all around. The table was set with beautiful linens and china. She served caviar and blini, smoked and marinated fish, the lightest scrambled eggs, *Gänseleberwurst* (smoked goose sausage), and two or three different kinds of ham: *Gekochter Schinken, Roher Schinken,* and *Bauernschinken.* There were always freshly baked pastries and breads. Everyone lingered at the table for hours with talk and talk and, at the end, even the newspaper was allowed with a glass of champagne and orange juice.

Skitch, with all his travels, can always find a good breakfast somewhere—even in the hinterlands. In fact, he'll often have a stack of pancakes with an egg on top for lunch or dinner. He also loves to cook breakfast, inventing new recipes and combinations all the time. Our favorite morning meals are simple. We cook eggs from the chickens next door and freshly made sausage from the farm up the road.

Skitch's Apple-Berry Pancakes

○

Bauernfrühstück

○

Breakfast in Bed

FAR LEFT: *This guest bed is in the loft above the Great Room, where a skylight provides good afternoon reading light and a warm glow for napping. The pillowcases are from Ruth's mother's trousseau.*
LEFT: *We warm up this corner for Skitch's breakfast with a fire in the Garrison stove.* ABOVE: *Sausage, bacon, and apple-berry compote are prepared at the kitchen stove.*

Skitch's Apple-Berry Pancakes

Both of us relish winter mornings, when Skitch has time to make pancakes on top of the wood-burning Garrison stove in the kitchen.

ABOVE: *Performing artists live and eat on unpredictable schedules—sometimes no schedule at all. Here, Skitch takes time to make pancakes for us on the Garrison. After this 2:00 P.M. ''breakfast,'' he's off to Carnegie Hall.*

1½ cups all-purpose flour
1 teaspoon salt
3 tablespoons sugar
1¾ teaspoons baking powder
2 large eggs, lightly beaten
1¾ cups buttermilk
3 tablespoons unsalted butter, melted
Vegetable oil, for cooking
Apple-berry compote (see recipe below)
Country sausage and bacon (see recipe, page 83)

Sift the dry ingredients into a medium bowl. Make a well in the center and fill with eggs, buttermilk, and melted butter. Stir until just blended. A few lumps don't matter.

Heat a skillet or griddle until hot (test by dropping a few drops of water on the surface; if water sputters, the griddle is perfect). Brush with a thin coating of oil. Drop 2 ladles of batter onto the griddle, enough to make two 4-inch pancakes. Cook until small bubbles appear on the top, then turn and cook on the other side until golden. Repeat the process until all batter is used. Keep cooked pancakes warm in a 200° F. oven in layers separated by a tea towel. Serve with apple-berry compote and country sausage and bacon.

Serves 4.

Apple-Berry Compote

The look of this compote adds to the pleasure of eating it. Be a little careful as you mix and stir so that your fruit remains firm.

4 McIntosh apples, peeled, cored, and sliced in ¼-inch rounds
Juice of 1 lemon
2 teaspoons unsalted butter
1½ teaspoons sugar
½ teaspoon ground cinnamon
2 10-ounce jars lingonberries or sweetened cooked cranberries

Winter

Place the apples in a large bowl and sprinkle with the lemon juice.

Melt the butter in a medium skillet or saucepan over medium heat. Add the apples and turn carefully until well coated with butter. Cook, without stirring, until apples are barely soft, about 3 minutes. Sprinkle with sugar and cinnamon and turn once. Allow to cool slightly, then gently fold in the berries. Serve warm over pancakes, and refrigerate any remaining compote in a glass jar with a tight-fitting lid.

Serves 4.

Country Sausage and Bacon

    1 **pound country sausage**
    10 **strips thickly sliced bacon**

Separate the sausage into 8 equal portions and shape into patties. Heat griddle or skillet until hot. Cook the patties until well browned, about 4 minutes on each side. Drain on paper towels and keep warm in a 200° F. oven.

In the same skillet, cook the bacon until crisp. Drain on paper towels and serve alongside apple-berry pancakes.

Serves 4.

LEFT: *Pancakes with bacon, sausage, and fruit compote are served in the warm corner near the stove.*

Bauernfrühstück

A farmer's breakfast! Ruth's great uncle had a farm near the Czechoslovakian border, and she spent many summers there with her cousins and cousins of cousins. Because she was an only child, these were the only times that she got to sit at the table with fifteen or twenty people and share food farmstyle—passing plates full of Bauernfrühstück, *dunking into large bowls of farmer cheese and onions, digging into an* Eintopf *at evening meal. There was a coal stove on the farm, always fired, with something always cooking. Farmhands and family often ate together. It was in the company of her large extended family that Ruth first experienced the joy of eating. And the food she devoured so enthusiastically with her cousins is really the food she prepares now.*

We recently served this breakfast for ourselves and two good friends. It's fun making this for friends—they can sit and watch you put it all together, or, if they sleep late, you can put it all together early, except for the eggs, and keep it warm. This can also make an excellent hearty brunch or supper.

3 tablespoons unsalted butter
8 ounces firm country sausage, sliced in ¼-inch rounds
8 ounces lean double-smoked bacon, diced
8 baking potatoes, sliced in ⅛-inch rounds
2 onions, diced
½ teaspoon salt
½ teaspoon freshly ground black pepper
2 teaspoons dried marjoram
1 green bell pepper, seeded and finely diced
1 cup chopped fresh parsley
9 large eggs, well beaten
8 ripe plum tomatoes, cut in half lengthwise
8 ounces mozzarella cheese, sliced

Melt 1 tablespoon butter in a large (14-inch) skillet over medium heat. Add the sausage and bacon and cook, turning often, until browned. Transfer sausage and bacon to a plate and melt remaining butter in the same skillet over medium heat. Add the potatoes and cook, turning often, until browned and just barely tender, about 15 minutes. Add the onions and cook until soft, about 5 to 8 minutes. Return sausage and bacon to the skillet and add the salt, pepper, marjoram, green pepper, and parsley. Stir gently until well combined. Continue to cook over medium heat for 1 minute. Gently fold in the eggs until fully combined. Cook for 1 minute, remove from heat, and let stand for 3 minutes (eggs will continue to cook gently off the heat). Serve right from the skillet, with fresh tomato halves and mozzarella cheese on the side.

Serves 4, with enough leftovers for another meal.

Our Local Farmers

We're fortunate to have good local farmers here, which means good meat, vegetables, fruits, and cheese. We hope that one of the trends of the future is the return of small local farmers who produce one or two good products. The people we know and meet through The Silo Store want more choice and more control over the quality of what they buy.

Jim and Nancy Dougherty are neighbors who have spent ten years developing a small pig farm they've named the Egg and I. Using some modern techniques and old-fashioned common sense, they've been able to raise pigs in a quiet, clean, and stress-free environment. (The only sounds other than the occasional car on the road are the crow of a rooster or the whoosh of the wind.) When the Doughertys' pigs go to market, they have been raised on nothing but first-class chemical- and additive-free food.

Both Jim and Nancy, like the two of us, are transplanted urbanites. Their farm, for now, consists of one house, two pig barns, a large garden tended by Nancy in spring and summer, and a small retail shop with a hand-painted sign out front that reads THE PORK SCHOP. This is where we buy our sausage, ham, and bacon—and the most delicious pork loin we've ever roasted.

ABOVE: *A big, heavy skillet is ideal for cooking and serving this breakfast.*

BELOW: *This is a meaty breakfast served in bowls. Ruth found fresh plum tomatoes at the local grocery store and added them to the meal as a side dish. Cilantro garnishes the Virgin and Bloody Marys.*

Breakfast in Bed

Ruth is an early bird, while Skitch likes to sleep in. When she hears the radio, she knows he's about ready to enter the day, and she'll bring him coffee with honey. But on concert days, she'll bring him breakfast in bed. It makes him smile and it's a good beginning to a very long day. We also like to prepare this breakfast tray for guests who stay in the loft above the great room.

WINTER FRUIT PLATE

EGG IN THE HOLE

ABOVE: *Skitch taught Ruth how to make egg in the hole early in their marriage. A thick slice of nutty or multi-grain bread ensures the best flavor and a sturdy nest for the egg.*
RIGHT: *Ruth works early mornings at her desk beneath the loft. Her view out the original barn window provides a secret pleasure—watching Keiran and Kythera run across the field to catch the school bus.*

OPPOSITE, TOP: *Sometimes, our breakfast consists simply of strawberries dipped in sour cream and dusted with cinnamon and sugar.*

OPPOSITE, BOTTOM: *At breakfast time, the cats press against the glass door until they get their meals served on toy trucks.*

Winter Fruit Plate

This makes a wonderful dinnertime dessert as well. It's very pretty and comforting when served on warm plates.

    8 dried apricots
    4 dried figs
    1 ripe Bartlett pear
    1 tablespoon raspberry syrup*

Place the apricots and figs in a small bowl, cover with water, and soak overnight. Drain.

Roughly peel the pear, leaving the stem and some of the peel on the bottom end. Place pear in a vegetable steamer with a small amount of water. Heat water to boiling, cover, and steam 8 to 10 minutes. Add the apricots and figs and steam 2 minutes more.

Meanwhile, heat the syrup in a small saucepan until just warm.

Arrange the fruit on a warm plate and drizzle with raspberry syrup. (Or spoon the syrup onto the plate and arrange the fruit on top.)

Serves 1.

*Fruit syrups are available in most fine food shops. In this recipe, maple syrup is a good substitute.

Egg in the Hole

    2 tablespoons (¼ stick) unsalted butter
    4 ounces Canadian bacon
    1 slice coarse whole-grain bread (cut it yourself from a whole
        loaf, if you can)
    1 large egg
    1 teaspoon honey, warmed

Melt 1 teaspoon of the butter in a skillet over medium heat. Add the bacon and cook until lightly browned. Remove from skillet and keep warm in a 200° F. oven.

Using a 2½-inch biscuit cutter, cut a hole in the center of the bread slice. Melt 2 teaspoons butter in another skillet over medium heat. Add the bread and sauté in the butter until browned, about 2 minutes. Turn the bread over and melt the remaining butter in the center hole in the bread. Crack the egg into the hole, cover, and cook over medium-low heat until yolk is set, about 4 minutes. Transfer with a spatula to a heated plate and drizzle with honey. Add the bacon to the plate and serve immediately.

Serves 1.

Spring

Yes, before spring arrives, there is a mud season and, yes, it's no fun.

SPRING

The dogs come in leaving trails. Boots have to come off every time we enter the house. A mudroom is a must—a corner with a big horse-feeding tub to catch the footwear. Walking up the mountain is inspiring nevertheless. We don't care how deep we sink in or how much the dogs roll and roll. The day finally comes when the brook starts running, a cheerful sound. Ice melts, leaving different designs every day.

The air is fresh. There's still a little frost some mornings, but often it's so warm at lunchtime that we can sit in the sun and soak it up. Then, before we know it, from up at the pond, we hear the two mallard ducks who make their way back to us each year. And, in the 1836 Barnyard, the first fat dandelion appears.

Most people consider this just a weed. Not us. We love dandelions through all their stages—the big fat buds, the rich yellow blooms, and the puff balls of seed. Ruth still blows the seeds away as she did as a child, the milk dripping from the stem. We love their color, strength, and persistence. We even like the shape and taste of the leaves. That's why we called our first restaurant Daly's Dandelion.

After the first appearance of the dandelion comes the glory of the forsythia up and down the road and the masses of daffodils—all yellows with orange centers, two yellows in one, and the almost pure whites. The tulips come up by the dozens in pink, red, yellow, and white. Skitch's oldest friend, Richard Jones, who lives in Mississippi, sends us bulbs every year—a wonderful gift of ongoing joy.

We walk by the pond and the new tadpoles dip and dive for safety. The cows come out of winter quarters to join spring in the pastures below our barn; we can watch them from our window above. The horses finally shed their thick winter coats. And the birds—robins and finches—return to the tallest trees next to the barn for their spring habitat. Everything is finally awake.

PRECEDING PAGES: *We planted three crabapple trees more than twenty years ago. The only fruit they bear are these glorious blossoms.* ABOVE: *This is the brook near the path up the mountain that Ruth hikes each morning. Not long after the first thaw has begun, Isabelle indulges.*

TOP: *We've planted so many daffodils that they come up in expected as well as unexpected places.*
CENTER: *Violets increase every year, making carpets around trees and bunching between stones on the walks.* ABOVE: *For us, the dandelion is not a weed to be exterminated: it is the proclamation of spring and a protected species.* RIGHT: *The wagon in The Silo barnyard will be cleaned and used as a buffet table at The Silo Gallery spring opening.*

Spring

We love walking to the pond while the crabapples are in bloom.
R I G H T : *The sun is warm and Jupiter's winter coat is almost shed.*

Einsiedel Anniversary
Dinner

•

Easter Sunday Buffet

•

Guest-of-Honor
Cocktail Party

•

Spring Fling:
Ice Cream Indulgences

•

Midday Meal on the
Deck for Six

•

Gone Fishing

•

Last-Day-of-Spring
Afternoon Tea

Einsiedel Anniversary Dinner

*H*ildegard and Kurt Einsiedel were married on March 21, 1929—the beginning of spring. Each year we celebrate with an anniversary dinner, as they did—it's become a tradition. Ruth's mother had a special way of entertaining. Her style, in fact, is still remembered with enthusiasm by Ruth's group of kindergarten friends who still meet yearly to visit, talk, and look back. It's amazing how a fifth-birthday celebration can be recalled so clearly because everybody ate grown-up food on the best china and drank peach champagne (a nonalcoholic invention) in crystal glasses. And each child was told to hold his or her glass on the very bottom to get the clearest sound when toasting. They all still do. Ruth's father did not cook, but he loved food and was an adventurous eater, enjoying game, fish, and foods from across the borders of Hungary, Italy, and Greece. Kurt left for the war in September 1939 and didn't return until 1945. Their home was destroyed but some of the treasures survived in safe storage at Ruth's great-uncle's farm in Eichigt on the Czechoslovakian border.

We have everything that survived in our 1836 Barn. Among the family treasures are hand-embroidered tablecloths, monogrammed linen dish towels, hand-cut crystal, a Meissen coffee set, and an almost complete 1928 Rosenthal dinner service in white, blue, and gold. We bring it all out for the anniversary dinner.

Asparagus Soup

o

Medallions of Veal in Gravy with Morels

o

Green Beans

o

Windbeutel

A B O V E : *Ruth's mother's favorite way to serve medallions of veal was over freshly made* Spätzle *topped with toasted bread crumbs.*

L E F T : *Our English oak table on wheels lets us move dinner wherever we want. Here, we catch the afternoon light for an early dinner in the Great Room. Silver trays, dessert, and a coffee service sit atop a German farm wagon.*

ABOVE: *Ruth's collection of silver napkin rings holds her mother's napkins and a sprig from a branch of apple blossoms.*

Asparagus Soup

One of the most versatile foods in our pantry is white asparagus. This soup takes very little time to make, is wonderfully satisfying, and was Ruth's mother's favorite.

> 3 12-ounce jars white asparagus
> 2 tablespoons (¼ stick) unsalted butter
> 3 tablespoons all-purpose flour
> 4 cups chicken broth
>   Salt
> 6 sprigs fresh dill
>   Paprika crispbread (see recipe below)

Drain the liquid from the asparagus, reserving 2 cups. Cut the top 2½ inches off the asparagus. Reserve stalks for another meal and set liquid and tops aside. (Or, if you want a heartier, more filling soup, cut the spears in thirds and use the entire asparagus.)

Melt the butter in the top of a double boiler over hot water. Add the flour and whisk until mixture thickens, about 1 minute. Gradually whisk in the broth and the reserved asparagus liquid and salt to taste. Continue to cook, whisking often, until mixture is thick, about 5 minutes. Add the asparagus and remove pot from heat. Let stand until asparagus is warmed through, about 2 minutes. Serve garnished with sprigs of dill. Pass paprika crispbread on the side.

Serves 6.

Paprika Crispbread

> 1 baguette French bread
> 2–3 tablespoons unsalted butter, softened
>   Hot Hungarian paprika

Slice the baguette into thin rounds. Butter each round and sprinkle lightly with paprika. Place rounds in toaster oven until very crisp. Serve with asparagus soup.

Serves 6.

Spring

Medallions of Veal in Gravy with Morels

Here's an example of making a change in one of our favorite recipes in order to accommodate healthier life-styles. We have always prepared this recipe with cognac, but when we substituted the juice from the morels for the spirits, it gave this dish a divine flavor. It was terrific! We served this with Spätzle.

  1 ounce dried morels
  8 veal medallions, each about 1½ inches thick
    Salt and freshly ground black pepper
  2 tablespoons plus 2 teaspoons all-purpose flour
  3 tablespoons unsalted butter
  3 shallots, finely chopped
  2 cups anniversary veal stock (see recipe, page 98)
  1 cup half and half
  1 teaspoon fresh marjoram, or ½ teaspoon dried
  1 recipe *Spätzle* (see recipe, page 65)

Place the morels in a small bowl, cover with water, and soak overnight. Strain and reserve 1 cup of the liquid. Cut each morel in half.

Pound each veal medallion lightly with a meat mallet. Combine a pinch each of salt and pepper and 2 tablespoons flour; dredge the veal lightly in the seasoned flour. Melt the butter in a skillet or sauté pan over medium heat. Add the veal and cook until lightly browned, about 5 minutes on each side. Add the shallots, morels, and veal stock; simmer gently on low heat for 5 minutes.

Dissolve the 2 teaspoons flour in the liquid reserved from soaking the morels; gradually add the mixture to the skillet and simmer 5 minutes more. Transfer medallions to a plate and keep warm. Increase heat under skillet to medium-high and whisk in the half and half. Add marjoram and salt and pepper to taste. Heat to boiling, reduce heat, and simmer until sauce is reduced to desired consistency. Return veal to pan and allow it to warm through, about 3 minutes. Serve immediately over *Spätzle*.

Serves 6.

Open to Change

There's a forthrightness and honesty in the people around us these days—they let us know how their attitudes about food are changing. They want food spiced simply but interestingly. They are drinking and cooking with less or no alcohol. They are eating whole grains. They're looking to buy fresh, organic fruits and vegetables, natural grass-fed beef, free-range poultry, and veal from calves that haven't been abused by agribusiness procedures. And, because many of them are the people closest to us, we have *had* to be open to and even incorporate some of these changes in our own way of cooking and entertaining.

Frankly, we're surprised and happy about the changes. We never would have thought that we would let ourselves do things differently. To prepare sauces and gravies once laced with cognac, we substitute broths, vegetable stock, or spices and have been delighted with the results.

Einsiedel Anniversary Dinner

Anniversary Veal Stock

Ruth tries never to be without stock on hand in the freezer or refrigerator. Making a stock now is second nature to her; she'll put one on to simmer, using a bone she's saved, when she's just working around the house. The cooking smells alone make her happy. Ham, vegetables, fish—especially smoked fish—all make great stocks. Most keep up to six months in the freezer.

2½ pounds veal knuckles
2 carrots
2 stalks celery
1 bay leaf
1 leek, rinsed well
1 clove garlic, peeled and bruised
¼ teaspoon salt
4 black peppercorns
1 onion
4 quarts water

Combine all ingredients in a large pot. Heat to boiling, reduce heat, and simmer 2 hours.

Makes about 8 cups.

Green Beans

2 pounds fresh green beans, trimmed
1 tablespoon unsalted butter, softened
Salt and freshly ground black pepper
¾ cup blanched sliced almonds, toasted

Cook the beans in boiling salted water until just crisp and tender, about 3 minutes; drain. Toss with butter. Add salt and pepper to taste. Toss in most of the almonds, then garnish with remaining almonds.

Serves 6.

Windbeutel

Windbeutel *means bag of air. These are very light pastry puffs, a traditional dessert at the German table.*

- 1 cup plus 2 tablespoons milk
- 4 tablespoons (½ stick) unsalted butter
- ½ teaspoon sugar
  Pinch of salt
- 4 ounces (1 cup less 3 tablespoons) all-purpose flour
- 5 large eggs
- 1 cup heavy cream
- 1 ounce (¼ cup) confectioners' sugar, plus extra for finishing

Preheat the oven to 425° F. Grease a baking sheet and set aside.

Combine the milk, butter, sugar, and salt in a medium saucepan and heat to boiling. Remove from heat and beat in the flour. Return to medium heat and cook until dough is dry and breaks free of sides of pan. Transfer to a bowl and add the eggs one at a time, beating well after each addition. Continue beating until mixture has a waxy consistency. Transfer mixture to a pastry bag fitted with a large star-shaped tip.

Pipe six 2-inch rounds of dough onto the prepared baking sheet. Each round should be 1 inch high. Bake until lightly brown, about 20 minutes. Reduce heat to 375° F. and continue baking until cream puffs are firm, about 12 minutes more. Remove the baking sheet and immediately turn oven off. Pierce the side or bottom of each *Windbeutel* with the point of a sharp knife to allow steam to escape. Place the *Windbeutels* on a rack, then place the rack in the oven with the door ajar until they are dried out, about 15 minutes. Remove the rack and allow to cool completely.

Meanwhile, whip the cream with the confectioners' sugar until stiff peaks form, then transfer to a pastry bag fitted with a large star-shaped tip.

Cut off the top third of the *Windbeutel* with a serrated knife. Remove any moist dough from the center of the bottom portion with a spoon. Pipe whip cream into the bottom part of the *Windbeutel*, to extend ½ inch above the cut edge. Replace the top and sprinkle with confectioners' sugar.

Makes 6 puffs.

B E L O W : *The stairs to the loft above the Great Room are put to use to hold a coffeepot and plates. Silver trays span the edges of the farm wagon, which is filled with geraniums.*

Easter Sunday Buffet

When our children were little, we spent Easters skiing at Sugarbush, Vermont, with friends and their families. There was so much fun going on—games, races, egg hunts up the mountain—that a come-and-go buffet was ideal for Easter Sunday. We set a table with plenty of food that could hold all afternoon, tasting great piping hot or at room temperature. All snow revelers—kids and adults alike—could eat whenever they wanted to between runs and races.

Nowadays, eggs are hidden here along stretches of stone walls, and our grandchildren and godchildren hunt for them. But the traditional Sugarbush buffet still guarantees our grown-up children and their families, plus our extended family of neighbors, unhurried pleasure long into the day.

Roasted Buttermilk-Rosemary
Leg of Lamb with
Fresh Mint Sauce

o

Radishes and Scallions with
Avocado-Horseradish Dip

o

Boiled Mini-Potatoes with
Chopped Scallions

o

Steamed Asparagus Bundles
with Chopped Egg
Vinaigrette

o

Sour-Creamed Spinach

o

Chris DeFelice's Easter Bread
and
Whole-Bunny Butter

o

Easter Pavlova with Pistachio
and Strawberry Ice Cream
and Sour Cherries

LEFT: *We celebrate Easter in Skitch's former studio, which is now Ruth's office, because the collection of carousel animals lives there. Our favorite is the rabbit.* ABOVE: *At the count of three, each child races to the walls, which are dotted with eggs, in order to be the one who finds and captures the most.* ABOVE, RIGHT: *A bleeding heart plant near the white wall by The Silo entrance grows larger each spring.*

Roasted Buttermilk-Rosemary Leg of Lamb with Fresh Mint Sauce

1   7½-pound leg of lamb, trimmed, with bone in
1   lemon, cut in half
6   cloves garlic, peeled and bruised
1   teaspoon salt
1   teaspoon freshly ground black pepper
8   large sprigs fresh rosemary, or 1 tablespoon dried
1   quart buttermilk
2   tablespoons (¼ stick) unsalted butter
10 shallots, peeled and finely chopped
1   teaspoon chopped fresh marjoram, or ½ teaspoon dried
12 medium mushrooms, halved
    Fresh mint sauce (see recipe, page 103)

Rub the lamb with lemon halves, squeezing the juice as you rub. Then rub with 1 or 2 garlic cloves and sprinkle with salt and pepper. Place lamb in a large ceramic crock or a large, heavy plastic bag. Add remaining garlic, rosemary, and buttermilk to crock or bag and cover or seal tightly. Marinate 8 hours (turning often if in a crock; if in a plastic bag, squeeze the liquid around the lamb often).

Preheat the oven to 325° F. If you are using a convection oven, which we prefer for this recipe, preheat it to 300° F. Remove the lamb from the marinade and place it on a rack in a roasting pan. Pour marinade plus 1 cup of water into the pan. Roast until the internal temperature registers 155° F. on a meat thermometer, about 2½ hours (2 hours in a convection oven). Let rest 15 minutes before carving.

Meanwhile, melt the butter in a medium saucepan. Add the shallots and cook until soft, about 2 minutes. Add the marjoram and the mushrooms and cook 3 minutes more.

Carve and serve the lamb with the mushrooms and fresh mint sauce on the side.

Serves 8, with enough leftovers for another meal.

OPPOSITE, TOP: *We buy Easter lilies from Joan and John Creedon in nearby Bantam. What we don't give away we plant by the tobacco barn. In late summer they bloom again and then every year thereafter.*
OPPOSITE, BOTTOM: *Right outside the Main House, the daffodils are quick to bloom before the ground cover grows thick. Eventually, the ground cover will grow twice as high as the daffodils.*

LEFT: *Lamb with mushrooms and shallots is served on a copper tray. Mint growing in a rabbit cachepot is for the true mint lovers in our family, who add the fresh-picked leaves to their own servings of meat and sauce.*
BELOW: *At Easter, potted flowering plants fill every space. Alma Mahler Henderson, our King Charles spaniel, fixes her gaze on an Easter egg.*

Fresh Mint Sauce

    4 tablespoons chopped fresh mint leaves
    ¼ cup hot water
    ¼ cup sugar
    ¾ cup malt vinegar

Combine the mint, water, and sugar in a small bowl. Stir until sugar is dissolved. Cool, then stir in the vinegar. Serve at room temperature.

Makes about 1 cup.

Easter Sunday Buffet

Radishes and Scallions with Avocado-Horseradish Dip

This will keep for a long time on the buffet if you place the bowl in a larger bowl of chopped ice.

> 5 tablespoons half and half
> 2 tablespoons lemon juice
> 2 teaspoons Dijon-style mustard
> 10 drops hot pepper sauce
> 1 ripe avocado, seeded, peeled, and sliced
> 2 teaspoons prepared horseradish
> 2 bunches radishes, trimmed
> 3 bunches scallions, trimmed

Combine the cream, lemon juice, mustard, and hot pepper sauce in a food processor or blender. Process or blend 30 seconds. Add the avocado, 1 slice at a time, pulsing each time until smooth. Add the horseradish and serve as dip for the vegetables.

Makes about 2 cups. Serves 8.

RIGHT: *With the service placed on basket trays, we can easily take our movable feast anywhere in the room or out onto the deck in the sunshine.*

Boiled Mini-Potatoes with Chopped Scallions

    5 pounds Florida Creamer potatoes
    ½ cup chopped scallions

Place potatoes in a large saucepan. Cover with water and heat to boiling. Remove from heat and allow to set 5 minutes. Drain and place in serving bowl. Sprinkle with scallions.

Serves 8.

Steamed Asparagus Bundles with Chopped Egg Vinaigrette

    48 fresh asparagus spears
     1 leek, rinsed well
     1 clove garlic, minced
    ½ teaspoon salt
    ½ teaspoon black pepper
       Dash of cayenne pepper
     6 tablespoons white-wine vinegar
       Juice of 1 lemon
     1 cup vegetable oil
     4 hard-boiled eggs, whites and yolks separated

Wash asparagus and trim ends so that all spears are the same length. Cut root end from leek and discard (or save for another recipe), then wash green ends and cut into eight ¼-inch strips. Using tongs, gently dip each strip into a deep pot of boiling water for 2 or 3 seconds.

Arrange asparagus in bundles of 6. Tie each bundle with 1 leek strip. Place bundles in a vegetable steamer (or, if you prefer, you can use a fish poacher) with a small amount of water. Heat water to boiling, cover, and steam until just tender, about 6–8 minutes. Remove bundles and place on serving platter.

Mash the garlic and the salt with the back of a spoon in a small bowl until smooth. Stir in the pepper, cayenne, vinegar, and lemon juice. Whisk in the oil. Crumble the egg yolks and whisk into vinaigrette, then finely chop the egg whites and fold them in. Serve drizzled over the asparagus or pass in a separate bowl on the side.

Serves 8.

TOP: *By Easter, the apple tree by the Main House is bursting with the promise of summer fruit.* ABOVE: *Lambs' ears, another gift from nature, multiplies with no help from us.*

Sour-Creamed Spinach

    5 pounds fresh spinach, washed, stems removed
    ¼ cup vegetable oil
    3 large onions, finely diced
    2 teaspoons all-purpose flour
    1 8-ounce container sour cream
    ½ teaspoon freshly grated nutmeg
    ¼ teaspoon freshly ground black pepper
    1 14-ounce can whole beets, cut into julienne

Cook the spinach in ¼ cup of boiling water for 3 minutes. Transfer to a food processor or blender and pulse until roughly chopped, about 2 or 3 seconds. Set aside.

Heat the oil in a large saucepan over medium-high heat until hot. Add the onions and sauté until soft. Add the flour and stir until absorbed. Add the spinach and toss until well combined. Stir in the sour cream, nutmeg, and pepper. Serve warm or at room temperature, garnished with beets.

Serves 8.

Chris DeFelice's Easter Bread and Whole-Bunny Butter

Chris is a long-time friend, neighbor, and dauntless cook. We have never seen her too tired to put a meal together, nor have we seen her fazed when extra people show up at dinnertime. She and her husband, Michael, and their children, Ryan and Mia, are permanent residents of Hunt Hill's 1836 farmhouse. Our families are always combining for holidays, everydays, anydays! Whatever the occasion, Chris is apt to contribute some delectable edible.

    1 package (¼ ounce) active dry yeast
    3 tablespoons warm water (105°–115° F.)
    4 ounces (½ cup plus 4 teaspoons) sugar
    ½ teaspoon salt
    3 teaspoons crushed cardamom seeds
    2 large eggs, beaten
    8 tablespoons (1 stick) unsalted butter, melted and
        cooled
    1 cup milk, scalded and cooled
      Zest of 1 large orange

Up to 20 ounces (4 cups) all-purpose flour
1 egg yolk
1 tablespoon milk
Poppy seeds
¾ pound (3 sticks) unsalted butter, softened

Dissolve the yeast in the warm water in a small bowl. Let stand 10 minutes, then transfer to a larger bowl. Add the sugar, salt, cardamom, beaten eggs, melted butter, scalded milk, and orange zest; mix well. Gradually stir in enough of the flour to form a fairly stiff dough. Place dough on a lightly floured surface and knead until smooth. Place dough in a greased bowl, cover with a towel, and let rise in a warm place until doubled in volume, about 2 hours.

Punch down dough and divide into 2 equal portions. Divide each portion into thirds. Roll each third on a lightly floured surface to form a strand 18 × 24 inches long. Braid the strands from the center out to the ends. Place braided loaf on a lightly greased baking sheet and repeat the process with the remaining dough. Place the other loaf on the baking sheet, cover with a towel, and let rise in a warm place 2 hours.

Preheat the oven to 350° F. Beat the egg yolk with 1 tablespoon milk in a small bowl. Brush each loaf with egg wash, sprinkle with poppy seeds, and bake until bread is golden and shining, about 30 minutes.

Meanwhile, press the softened butter into a medium-size rabbit-shaped candy mold. Place in the freezer for 30 minutes. Just before serving, unmold by dipping mold quickly into very hot water. Invert onto a serving plate and serve with bread.

Makes 2 loaves.

BELOW: *Dimitri carefully explores the possibilities. Leaving food unattended is always a bit of a risk.*

Easter Pavlova with Pistachio and Strawberry Ice Cream and Sour Cherries

You can be very creative with this pavlova. Shape it any way you like prior to baking—a stork for a baby shower, a boat for a bon voyage, a flag for the Fourth of July, and so on. This is the only course in our Easter feast that has to be devoured immediately. Pavlova, an Australian delight, is usually filled with fresh fruit Down Under. But we prefer to be a bit un-Australian and fill it with ice cream.

    4 large egg whites
      Pinch of salt
    8 ounces (1 cup plus 2 tablespoons) superfine sugar
    ½ teaspoon vanilla extract
    1 teaspoon lemon juice
    1 tablespoon cornstarch
    1 quart pistachio ice cream, in a block
    1 quart strawberry ice cream
    1 23-ounce can sour cherries

Preheat the oven to 400° F. Line a baking sheet with parchment paper and set aside. Beat the egg whites with the salt until soft peaks form. Gradually add the sugar, vanilla, and lemon juice while continuing to beat until stiff but not dry. Fold in cornstarch. Using a spatula, spread half the batter on the baking sheet to form an oval 1½ inches thick. Build up the sides with the remaining batter to form outside edges.

Reduce heat to 250° F. and bake pavlova on the prepared baking sheet until puffed and golden, about 1½ hours. Turn oven off and allow pavlova to cool 1 hour in oven. Transfer carefully to a large serving platter.

Cut the pistachio ice cream into ¼-inch slices. Arrange slices around outside of pavlova. Fill center of pavlova with scoops of strawberry ice cream and garnish generously with cherries. Serve immediately.

Serves 8–10.

FAR RIGHT: *Our Australian daughter-in-law introduced us to her national dessert—pavlova. We made it in an egg shape and filled it with an American filling—ice cream and cherries. The bunnies were made by our cookie wizard, Sandy Daniels.*

Guest-of-Honor Cocktail Party

One late afternoon last spring, we invited fifty people for cocktails and food prior to a performance at the nearby Merryall Center for the Arts. The guest of honor was our friend Liz Smith, who was the featured speaker that night. We needed food that was prepared early, could be served at room temperature, and would be substantial. We chose to serve hearty open sandwiches—a good combination of dense bread (we used Holzofen Brot from Canada, available from The Silo Store) and tasty prepared meats and fresh vegetables. The party and Liz were both hits that night.

Cold Roast Loin of Pork
Sandwich
with Horseradish Apple
Butter

◦

Sandwich of Sarah Belk's
Spicy Marinated Beef

◦

Sandwich of Smoked Salmon
with Dill Butter

◦

Sliced Daikon Open
Sandwich

◦

Sandwich of Tomato with
Red and Green Basil

◦

Sandwich of Finely Sliced
Cucumber and Fresh Dill

LEFT: *Two unplanned last-minute additions to the party were fresh strawberries that Ruth couldn't resist buying from the grocer and a punch bowl of mint julep served in honor of the Kentucky Derby, which was running as the party got under way.* ABOVE: *Coleus adorn the tables and hearth during Liz's party. The dramatic lighting is provided by the spring afternoon sunshine.* RIGHT: *The hearth holds a silver tray with well-iced ''Stoly'' and silver shot glasses from Daly's. Each one is engraved with a date celebrating a special holiday or event. Again, the sun lights the scene.*

RIGHT: *Our old English laundry table easily accommodates the sandwich buffet of smoked salmon, pork and beef, tomato and basil, daikon, and cucumber and dill. Tomatoes and apples create an edible decoration.*

Cold Roast Loin of Pork Sandwich with Horseradish Apple Butter

	Juice of 3 oranges
	Juice of 1 lime
	Juice of 2 lemons
3	tablespoons chutney
1	cup prepared honey mustard
2	cups soy sauce
4	bay leaves
6	sprigs fresh rosemary, or 4 teaspoons dried
1	9-pound pork loin, with bone
2	red onions, quartered
4	carrots
2	leeks, rinsed well and quartered lengthwise
12–15	large slices dark bread
	Horseradish apple butter (see recipe, page 113)
6	radishes, trimmed and sliced very thin

Combine the orange, lime, and lemon juices with the chutney, honey mustard, soy sauce, bay leaves, and rosemary in a bowl. Mix well. Place pork and vegetables in a large ceramic dish or a large plastic bag. Add marinade, cover or seal, and refrigerate overnight. Remove pork and reserve marinade.

Preheat a convection oven to 300° F. (or a conventional oven to 350° F.). Place the vegetables in a roasting pan and add 2 cups water. Place the pork on a flat rack fitted over roasting pan and roast 1 hour. Baste the meat every 20 minutes with reserve marinade until its internal temperature reads 170° F. on a meat thermometer, about 3 hours. Let cool and slice thin.

Spread bread with the horseradish apple butter and cover with overlapping slices of pork. Dab lightly with more apple butter and cut in fourths or sixths, whichever makes an appropriate serving. Garnish with radish slices.

Serves 50.

Horseradish Apple Butter

8 ounces apple butter
3 tablespoons cream-style horseradish

Combine apple butter and horseradish in a small bowl.

Makes about 1 cup.

BELOW: *Pepper and sea salt are served in crocks. Curled scallions and cornichons garnish the pork.*

Sandwich of Sarah Belk's Spicy Marinated Beef

Sarah, who is senior editor at Bon Appetit, *prepared this recipe in her Southern Cooking class here at The Silo. It's always delighted us that the tastes and flavors of southern American cooking and German cooking are so similar. We were so taken with this beef that we had it frozen after Sarah's class (it keeps for six months) and decided to serve it at the party.*

A B O V E : *The Bohemian hand-cut glasses reside on the sill of this original 1836 Barn window. When the sun hits, the light behaves as if it were filtered through a prism, and colors spatter the room.*

        1 cup light brown sugar, firmly packed
        1 cup kosher (coarse) salt
        2 teaspoons freshly ground black pepper
        2 teaspoons ground allspice
        1 teaspoon freshly grated nutmeg
        ½ bay leaf, crumbled
     5½ pounds eye round of beef
        1 large onion, coarsely chopped
        2 medium carrots, peeled and coarsely chopped
        6 slices bacon
  12–15 large slices dark bread
        Mustardy mayonnaise (see recipe below)

Combine the brown sugar, salt, pepper, allspice, nutmeg, and bay leaf in a large bowl. Place the beef in a ceramic dish just large enough to hold it. Rub the meat with the dry mixture and place the onion and carrots directly over the meat. Cover and refrigerate 5 days, turning twice a day.

Preheat the oven to 275° F. Allow the meat to come to room temperature, then place it in a Dutch oven. Add the carrots, onion, marinade, and 1 cup water. Lay bacon strips over beef, cover, and roast until very tender, about 2 hours. Remove beef from liquid and allow it to come to room temperature. Wrap beef in plastic wrap and refrigerate 1 week.

Slice beef, either chilled or at room temperature, very thin. Spread the bread slices with the mustardy mayonnaise and cover with overlapping slices of beef. Cut in fourths or sixths, whichever makes an appropriate serving for your guests.

Serves 50.

Mustardy Mayonnaise

        1 cup mayonnaise
        3 tablespoons grainy mustard

Combing mayonnaise and mustard in a bowl; mix well. Serve with spicy beef sandwiches.

Makes 1¼ cups.

The Merryall Center and CD 199

The Merryall Center for the Arts is an intimate performance hall in a converted gristmill in New Milford, Connecticut. It's been a lively and important place for musical entertainment since 1951. Opera, chamber music, folk singing, lectures, dramatic readings, and piano concerts draw standing-room-only audiences from early May through Labor Day.

Alan Himelick, the program director, has become a friend, and he works hard and long to maintain the tradition set by the Merryall founders, among them Florence Eldridge and her husband, the celebrated actor Fredric March.

Each summer, Skitch offers the center the use of one of our two Steinway concert grand pianos. The one that works at Merryall is very special to us because it is signed by four of the Steinways. The other piano we are privileged to have is the Steinway CD (Concert Department) 199. Built by the Steinway Company in 1953, "Old 199," as it is affectionately called, was that company's proudest achievement. It was revered by classical pianists all over the world for its exceptional tone and light action. For twenty years, 199 was the first choice of symphony conductors, pianists, and recording artists. It traveled the country and worked for such greats as Eugene Ormandy, Dimitri Mitropoulos, Charles Munch, and Leonard Bernstein. And it was always the choice of our friend, the eminent concert pianist Gary Graffman. When Steinway decided to retire 199 from service, we bought it and gave it a home. Not long after its farewell recital at Carnegie Hall, 199 arrived at Hunt Hill Farm. And, except for an occasional special event away from home, Old 199 abides in the Great Room of our 1836 Barn, where it is always available to Skitch for his work and pleasure.

LEFT: *Both Steinways are at home in the Great Room. CD 199 is open and ready to be played. Skitch's studio grand temporarily holds family pictures.* ABOVE: *The small piano is a miniature replica of CD 199. Uncle John Steinway made it for Skitch's 60th birthday.*

Next-Day Potted Pâté

1 cup chopped leftover
   meats, such as
   spiced beef or pork
   loin
1 tablespoon unsalted
   butter, softened

Combine meat and butter in a food processor and process until smooth. Spoon into an 8- or 10-ounce crock. Serve with crackers or bread.

Serves 4–6.

Next-Day Sautéed White Radish

2 tablespoons (¼ stick)
   unsalted butter
2 cups white radish
   slices
1 cup chicken broth
1 tablespoon all-
   purpose flour

Melt the butter in a large skillet. Add the radish slices and sauté over medium-low heat.

   Meanwhile, heat the broth in a small saucepan until just warm. Add the flour and stir until blended. Add broth to skillet. Simmer gently 8–10 minutes, or until sauce is thickened.

Serves 2–4.

Sandwich of Smoked Salmon with Dill Butter

¾ cup (1½ sticks) unsalted butter, softened
¼ cup chopped fresh dill
¼ teaspoon lemon juice
12–15 slices coarse, heavy bread
4 pounds smoked salmon, thinly sliced
1 bunch fresh dill
6 lemons, sliced

Combine first 3 ingredients in a small bowl and mix well. Spread bread lightly with dill butter, then cover with overlapping slices of salmon. Cut in fourths or sixths, whichever is appropriate for your guests. Add sprigs of fresh dill for garnish. Serve with lemon.

Serves 50.

Sliced Daikon Open Sandwich

12–15 slices dark, heavy bread
8 tablespoons (1 stick) unsalted butter, softened
1 large white radish (daikon), peeled and very thinly sliced
¼ cup finely chopped fresh chives

Spread bread evenly with butter, then cover with overlapping slices of radish. Cut into fourths or sixths, whichever is appropriate for your guests. Sprinkle with chives.

Serves 50.

Sandwich of Tomato with Red and Green Basil

¾ cup (1½ sticks) unsalted butter, softened
¼ cup chopped fresh green basil
   Dash of hot pepper sauce

12–15 slices heavy, coarse bread
10 medium tomatoes, thinly sliced
1 small bunch red basil, leaves separated
1 small bunch green basil, leaves separated

Combine first 3 ingredients in a small bowl and mix well.

Spread bread evenly with butter, then cover with overlapping slices of tomato. Cut into fourths or sixths, whichever is appropriate for your guests. Garnish each portion with red and green basil leaves.

Serves 50.

Sandwich of Finely Sliced Cucumber and Fresh Dill

12–15 slices coarse, heavy bread
¾ cup (1½ sticks) lightly salted butter, softened
6 medium cucumbers, peeled and very thinly sliced
1 large bunch fresh dill, separated into sprigs

Spread the bread lightly with butter, then cover with overlapping slices of cucumber. Cut into fourths or sixths, whichever is appropriate for your guests. Garnish each with fresh dill.

Serves 50.

LEFT: *Knowing when sunlight shines into the room helps us enhance the look of the buffet. Even the parsley casts a shadow.* BELOW: *The green chip of light is from the crystal goblet in the window. Slices of daikon are sprinkled with chopped chives.*

Spring Fling:
Ice Cream Indulgences

*E*very spring, the New York Pops hosts a gala birthday celebration for itself. And although the event takes place in New York City at Carnegie Hall, many of the preparations are done right here on the farm. Our staff are very generous with their time. There are mailings, telephone calls, VIP invitations going out, and RSVPs coming in. Everyone wears at least three different hats. We all work in the office piled high with Silo material and New York Pops literature.

From February through May, the gala rules our lives. The pace gets hectic and wears on the good natures of the people who work here. So, around the time we're getting circles under our eyes and tempers are getting short, we clean off the old marble soda fountain, which by this time is totally camouflaged with posters, seating charts, and invitations, scoop up some wonderful ice creams and toppings, and take a spring break—a vital necessity more than an indulgence!

**Three Sundaes with
Three Sauces**

○

Strawberry-Stuffed Pizelles

FAR LEFT: *All the box seats for the New York Pops spring gala are finally sold, and the tickets are on their way to the patrons! We all deserve a treat.* LEFT: *Primroses grow in several pots. Later, we will plant them in the patch near the barbecue shed—a patch that naturally grows larger each year.* ABOVE: *No, we did not shoot these beautiful deer! They are remnants from The Mushroom, an antique shop Ruth owned once upon a time. Posters, designed by Paul Rigby, celebrate seasons of the New York Pops.*

Three Sundaes with Three Sauces

These look very festive when served in tulip glasses. You can use any good-quality brand of ice cream, or make your own. We serve these sundaes with Chocolate Lace, a Connecticut confection available at The Silo.

Hot Fudge Sundae

- 2 ounces unsweetened chocolate
- 1 tablespoon unsalted butter
- ⅓ cup strong hot coffee
- 1 cup sugar
- 2 tablespoons light corn syrup
- 4 drops almond extract or Amaretto liqueur
  Chocolate ice cream

Melt the chocolate with the butter in the top of a double boiler over simmering water. Stir in the coffee. Add the sugar and corn syrup and stir until smooth. Add the extract or liqueur just before serving hot over chocolate ice cream.

Serves 4–6.

Butterscotch Sundae

⅓ cup corn syrup
½ cup light brown sugar, finely packed
2 tablespoons (¼ stick) unsalted butter
⅓ cup heavy cream
Vanilla ice cream

Heat the corn syrup, brown sugar, and butter in the top of a double boiler over simmering water until smooth. Allow to cool slightly, then stir in the cream. Serve warm or cold over vanilla ice cream.

Serves 4–6.

White Chocolate Sundae

This is the kind of sauce that ladles on warm and hardens to a light shell. Fabulous and worth the effort! Note that this sauce will keep, but it must be reheated to be used.

8 ounces white chocolate
Strawberry ice cream

Grate the chocolate and place half of it in the top of a double boiler over simmering water. Stir until chocolate is melted and temperature reads 110° F. on a candy thermometer. Remove top of double boiler and set on a towel. Add remaining chocolate to the top of the double boiler, stirring until chocolate is completely melted and temperature has cooled to 75° F. Return to bottom half of double boiler and reheat over simmering water, stirring constantly, until temperature reads 89° F. Serve hot over strawberry ice cream.

Serves 4–6.

Strawberry-Stuffed Pizelles

This confection may intrigue you enough to invest in a pizelle iron, if you don't already have one. It's so easy to make these, and they are a special surprise at any party.

3 large eggs, lightly beaten
¾ cup sugar
½ teaspoon anise seeds
8 tablespoons (1 stick) unsalted butter, melted
1 teaspoon vanilla extract
1⅓ cups flour
2 teaspoons baking powder
2 pints fresh strawberries, hulled and halved
    Confectioners' sugar

BELOW: *Cast-iron chairs, which Ruth bought long before she met Skitch, make a perfect marriage with the old Marbledale soda fountain. A sign carved by a fan depicts Skitch at a saloon piano.*

Beat the eggs with the sugar in a medium bowl until light and cream colored. Add the anise, butter, and vanilla and beat until well blended. Sift the flour and baking powder into the egg mixture and beat until well blended. Fill a pastry bag fitted with a medium-size round tip with batter.

Heat the pizelle iron and pipe the batter onto the iron; bake according to manufacturer's directions.

Roll the pizelle into a cone shape while it's still very hot. Fill with strawberries and sprinkle with confectioners' sugar.

Serves 12.

Savory Pizelles

Simply leave out the sugar in the recipe, and add a little salt, pepper, and a ground herb to the batter. Then roll the pizelle and fill it with ham or asparagus. Or leave the pizelle flat and spoon chicken fricassee over the top. Add another pizelle layer and spoon more fricassee over the top. Invent your own.

Spring Fling: Ice Cream Indulgences

123

Midday Meal on the Deck for Six

*T*his is ideal to serve outdoors on the first warm day of the year. When spring first arrives at the farm, we scrub down the deck and furniture and bring out the potted geraniums, which spend the winter indoors, for their first taste of spring.

Cornish Hens with Wild Rice Stuffing

○

Peas in Lemon Mayonnaise

○

Salad of Arugula, Mushroom, Radish, and Goat Cheese

LEFT: *The geraniums that had been blooming indoors came out to the deck and inspired the table setting. Radishes perform as a centerpiece before being devoured.* ABOVE: *Groucho seems to sleep while preparations for dinner are made. If any food is left outdoors unattended, he is swift to strike.*

Cornish Hens with Wild Rice Stuffing

Nowadays, one can find fresh figs even in early spring. This would also taste wonderful with plumped dried figs.

6 1½-pound Cornish game hens
10 black peppercorns
1 large sprig fresh marjoram, or 2 teaspoons dried
2 5-ounce packages instant wild rice
4 cups turkey or chicken stock
1 tablespoon unsalted butter
1 teaspoon chopped fresh marjoram
1 tablespoon minced shallots
1 cup raisins
½ cup pine nuts
6 fresh figs, cut in half

Preheat the oven to 450° F. Remove the hearts, gizzards, and livers from the hens and reserve.

Make a bouquet garni by tying the peppercorns and marjoram together in a piece of cheesecloth.

Cook the wild rice in the stock with the bouquet garni according to package directions. Discard bouquet garni and set aside to cool.

Heat 2 cups of water to boiling in a small saucepan. Add the reserved hearts and gizzards, reduce heat, and simmer until they are softened, about 5 minutes. Set aside.

Melt the butter in a small skillet over medium heat. Add the hearts and gizzards and sauté 3 minutes; move to side of pan. Add the livers and sauté 2 minutes on each side. Add the chopped marjoram and shallots and cook 1 minute more. Remove from heat and allow to cool. Chop meat finely and reserve.

Combine the rice, chopped meat, raisins, and pine nuts in a large bowl and mix well. Fill each hen with about 1 cup of stuffing. Place a fig half in the neck cavity of each hen. Truss hens and place them on a rack in a large roasting pan (make sure hens are not touching). Roast 15 minutes, then reduce heat to 350° F. and roast 30 minutes more. Allow to sit 10 minutes before serving. Garnish with remaining figs.

Serves 6.

FAR RIGHT: *Cornish hens are roasted in an oven-to-table dish.*

Spring

126

ABOVE: *The peas and salad are served in Bennington pottery bowls.*

The Parade of the Plants

During the cold months, every nook and cranny of the barn and poolhouse is filled with pots of flowers and plants that we've moved indoors for warm-keeping—geraniums, petunias, a fifteen-year-old orange tree, and cacti. There are herbs in little and big pots: lemon sage, marjoram, tarragon, oregano, and peppermint. There are four hearty rosemary bushes—one for each kitchen at the farm to use. We've only lost two over recent winters because we let them dry out. But, from those, we saved the dry branches and Skitch used them in the coals for summertime barbecues; the herbal smoke is divine.

In those dark months indoors, all potted herbs and plants do double duty, quite often as a centerpiece or to provide fresh-cut flowers for the table. But, in spring, around the last day of May, when the warmth is here to stay, the parade of plants and flowers makes its way outdoors.

Peas in Lemon Mayonnaise

Sheila Lukins is a good friend and frequent teacher at The Silo. Here, her terrific lemon mayonnaise enhances fresh peas.

> 1 large egg
> 2½ tablespoons fresh lemon juice
> 1 tablespoon Dijon-style mustard
> ½ cup corn oil
> ½ cup olive oil
> Zest of 1 lemon
> Freshly ground black pepper
> 2 tablespoons chopped fresh dill
> 2½ pounds fresh peas, or 2 10-ounce packages frozen peas, thawed

Place the egg, lemon juice, and mustard in a food processor and process 15 seconds. With the machine still running, slowly add the oils. Process until thick. Transfer mixture to a bowl and gently fold in lemon zest, pepper to taste, and dill. Cover and chill at least 2 hours.

Place peas in a vegetable steamer with a small amount of water. Heat water to boiling, cover, and steam 3 minutes. Allow peas to cool slightly, then serve with lemon mayonnaise on the side or tossed thoroughly with the peas.

Serves 6.

Salad of Arugula, Mushroom, Radish, and Goat Cheese

     2 bunches arugula
    10 ounces fresh mushrooms, sliced
     6 radishes, sliced
    ¼ pound mild goat cheese
    ½ teaspoon Dijon-style mustard
     2 teaspoons balsamic vinegar
    ¼ cup olive oil
        Salt and freshly ground black pepper

Line a small salad bowl with arugula leaves. Arrange the mushrooms and radishes within it to suit the eye. Crumble the goat cheese in the center.

   Whisk the mustard, vinegar, and oil together in a small bowl. Add salt and pepper to taste. At the table, just before serving, pour dressing over salad, toss, and serve.

Serves 6.

BELOW LEFT AND ABOVE: *In spring, the Henderson car collection comes out of the barn. Skitch gave this 1930 Model A to Ruth on her fiftieth birthday. The 1972 Mercedes, also a gift, is the last model with an all-steel chassis. All cars are Skitch's favorite color—English racing green.*

ABOVE: *The dashboard of the Chevy truck awaits polishing.*

Gone Fishing

As the last bit of winter thaws from the pond, our grandson Keiran and our godson, Ryan, get their fishing poles ready. There are largemouth bass in the pond and the boys do manage to angle one or two, which they also manage to clean and cook for themselves. On these occasions, they've even been known to bring us a bite to sample. Sometimes it's 7:00 A.M. when they show up with their prize catch. It's usually only a bite, however, because the bass are rarely larger than six inches. We know there are older and larger bass in the pond, which will probably grow even older as they successfully avoid these fishermen. At any rate, it doesn't take the rest of us long to get into the fish-fry spirit. There's a brick barbecue grill that must be at least fifty years old outside the farmhouse next to the pond. After an appetizer of six-inch bass, there's nothing more satisfying than a big fish feast.

Stuffed and Grilled Red Snapper with Vegetables

o

Sour Cream–Horseradish Sauce

o

Quick Spinach Bread

FAR LEFT: *Sheba, our beauty, is a mysterious mix—collie? husky? She chews a stick at the foot of the feast. The day was warm enough to eat outside.* LEFT: *Keiran and Kythera head toward the mountain beyond the pond.* ABOVE: *An even bed of coals assures a perfectly cooked fish. Be patient: we wait for the appearance of glowing ashes.*

Stuffed and Grilled Red Snapper with Vegetables

Ask your fish merchant to bone the fish and leave it whole for you. A fish basket is perfect for grilling and great for serving. The Sour Cream–Horseradish Sauce (page 134) is a terrific accompaniment.

For the vegetables

- ½ medium head cauliflower, separated into florets
- 4 medium carrots, cut in thirds
- 2 ears corn, shucked and cut in thirds
- 9 Texas or white onions, halved
- 4 bay leaves
- ⅓ cup lemon-garlic vinegar*
- 6 small potatoes
- 1 large red bell pepper, seeded and cut into sixths
- 1 large green bell pepper, seeded and cut into sixths

Place the cauliflower, carrots, corn, and 12 onion halves in a vegetable steamer with water. Add bay leaves and lemon-garlic vinegar to the water. Heat to boiling, cover, and steam 8 minutes. Remove vegetables and set aside. Place potatoes in steamer, cover, and steam 15 minutes. Arrange vegetables, including peppers, in a lightly oiled grilling basket and set aside. Reserve remaining onion halves for garnish.

*Lemon-garlic vinegar is available in most fine food shops and at The Silo.

For the snapper

- 2 medium heads fennel, trimmed and peeled
- 2 medium leeks, trimmed, washed well, and quartered lengthwise
- 8 tablespoons (1 stick) unsalted butter
- 8 cloves garlic, peeled and bruised
- 6 fresh sage leaves
- ½ teaspoon freshly ground white pepper
- 1 lemon
  Salt
- 1 6-pound red snapper, boned and trimmed

FAR RIGHT: *Choose the freshest vegetables available and pre-steam them to keep them from drying.*

Place the fennel in a vegetable steamer with water. Heat to boiling, cover, and steam 5 minutes. Add the leeks and steam 3 minutes more. Remove vegetables. When fennel has cooled, slice it as thinly as possible. Set aside.

Spring

Melt the butter in a small saucepan and add the garlic, sage, white pepper, and juice from the lemon. Simmer gently until all ingredients are warmed through. Slice the lemon hulls into thin strips and set aside.

Prepare the coals and the grill. When coals are white-hot, brush the inside of fish generously with the butter mixture. Sprinkle with salt. Stuff the cavity with the sliced lemon, fennel, and leeks. Place in a lightly oiled fish grilling basket and grill over hot coals for 20 minutes each side. Ten minutes before fish is done, place the basket of vegetables on the grill and grill 5 minutes on each side. Transfer vegetables to a serving platter and garnish with the remaining onion halves. Serve the fish right from the basket.

Serves 6.

Sour Cream–Horseradish Sauce

> 1 small clove garlic, minced
> ½ teaspoon salt
> 1 16-ounce container sour cream
> 6 tablespoons grated fresh or prepared horseradish
> ½ teaspoon freshly ground white pepper
> 3 tablespoons chopped fresh chives

Mash the garlic and the salt together in a bowl with the back of a spoon until smooth. Add the sour cream, horseradish, and pepper and stir until well blended. Just before serving, fold in the chives.

Makes about 2½ cups.

Quick Spinach Bread

On some occasions, store-bought bread dough is just what we need for an easy outdoor meal.

> 2 10-ounce packages prepared bread dough (from refrigerator case in supermarket)
> 4 tablespoons (½ stick) unsalted butter, melted
> 1 10-ounce package frozen chopped spinach, thawed
> 1 red onion, peeled and finely chopped
> 1 teaspoon freshly ground black pepper

Preheat the oven to 350° F. Roll out the 2 packages of dough separately on a lightly floured surface according to package directions. Brush each surface with one-fourth of the butter. Sprinkle each evenly with spinach, onion, and pepper. Roll the dough up to form 2 loaves, then make small diagonal cuts in the top of each and brush with remaining melted butter. Place loaves on a lightly greased baking sheet and bake until golden, about 25 minutes.

Serves 6.

BELOW: *As the weather warms up, lemon water is a must in the Henderson household. We keep a pitcher in the refrigerator at all times. This one rests on a French marble table.*

OPPOSITE, TOP: *We serve the fish right in its basket. The vegetable-basket top doubles as a grate to keep the bread warm.* OPPOSITE, MIDDLE: *The vegetables are served on an Arthur Court platter and garnished with fresh tomatoes and Texas onions.* OPPOSITE, BOTTOM: *Basket trays are practical for outdoors, since they're light and roomy. Weave the napkin in place.*

Gone Fishing

Last-Day-of-Spring Afternoon Tea

When spring and summer meet, we are anxious to be outdoors as much as possible. We love to break out the white linens and the silver, and get in the mood for the season ahead, anticipating all the special places where we will sit, talk, eat, and enjoy ourselves— places where the phone won't reach us. One favorite spot of ours is under the big tree overlooking the horse pasture. Salome and Jupiter, our two Morgans, love to nuzzle in.

Cinnamon-Pecan Tea Biscuits

○

Lemon Pound Cake

○

Honey Raisin Loaf Bread

○

Blueberry Cornbread

○

Irish Soda Scones

FAR LEFT: *A warm morning rain almost washed out our plans for an afternoon tea. But when the sun came out, so did the tea service, coffeepot, and cakes. Salome and Jupiter await the guests.* LEFT: *Uneaten grass on the other side of the fence is thick by late spring.* ABOVE: *The Silo cats, who live in the former milk house, almost never accept a newcomer but take turns in caring for their combined litters. With kittens in day care, moms hunt and play.*

ABOVE: An English oak vitrine holds the Einsiedel Meissen coffee set, hand-cut crystal from the Böhmer-wald, and English fruit plates.

Cinnamon-Pecan Tea Biscuits

  4 tablespoons (½ stick) unsalted butter, softened
10 ounces (2 cups) all-purpose flour
  ½ ounce (4 teaspoons) baking powder
    Pinch of salt
1½ ounces (¼ cup) sugar
  1 large egg
  ½ cup milk
  1 ounce (⅓ cup) chopped pecans
  2 tablespoons sugar mixed with 1 tablespoon ground
    cinnamon

Preheat the oven to 325° F. Grease a baking sheet and set aside.

With a pastry blender, cut the butter into the flour until mixture is the texture of coarse crumbs. Add remaining ingredients except sugar-cinnamon mixture and combine until the consistency of soft dough. Sprinkle a flat surface with the sugar-cinnamon mixture and roll out the dough to a ¾-inch thickness. Cut the dough with a 2-inch biscuit cutter and place biscuits on prepared sheet. Bake until golden, about 30 minutes.

Makes about 15 biscuits.

Lemon Pound Cake

  6 tablespoons (¾ stick) unsalted butter, softened
  5 ounces (¾ cup) sugar
  2 large eggs
  ⅓ cup milk
    Juice and zest of 1 lemon
  ½ teaspoon vanilla extract
  5 ounces (1 cup plus 6 tablespoons) cake flour, sifted
  ½ teaspoon baking powder
    Pinch of salt

Preheat the oven to 325° F. Lightly grease a 7 × 3-inch loaf pan and set aside. Beat butter and sugar together in a bowl until light in color. Add eggs, one at a time, beating 1 minute after each addition. Gradually add milk, lemon juice and zest, and vanilla. Add flour, baking powder, and salt and beat 1 minute. Pour batter into the prepared pan and bake until a toothpick inserted in the center comes out clean, about 1 hour and 15 minutes.

Makes 1 loaf.

Honey Raisin Loaf Bread

½ cup plus 1 tablespoon milk

1½ ounces (½ cup) rolled oats

2 ounces (5 tablespoons) brown sugar

2 teaspoons honey

1 large egg

3 tablespoons vegetable oil

2 ounces (6 tablespoons) all-purpose flour

¾ teaspoon baking powder

¼ teaspoon baking soda

Pinch of salt

⅓ cup raisins

Preheat the oven to 325° F. Lightly grease a 7 × 3-inch loaf pan, line the bottom with wax paper, grease and flour the paper, and set aside. Combine all the ingredients in a large bowl and mix well. Pour batter into the prepared pan and bake until golden and center is firm to the touch, 50–60 minutes.

Makes 1 loaf.

BELOW: *Starched linens and home-baked tea cakes and breads turn the time back for us and our guests.*

Blueberry Cornbread

2½ ounces (5 tablespoons) sugar

¼ cup vegetable oil

3 ounces (⅔ cup) all-purpose flour

3 ounces (½ cup plus 1 tablespoon) cornmeal

4 ounces (½ cup) dairy sour cream

½ teaspoon baking soda

Pinch of salt

2 large eggs

1 cup blueberries, washed and picked over

Preheat the oven to 300° F. Lightly grease a 7 × 3-inch loaf pan, line the bottom with wax paper, grease and flour the paper, and set aside. Combine all ingredients except the blueberries in a large bowl and mix well. Pour batter into the prepared pan, sprinkle with the berries, and push berries into the batter with your fingertips. Bake until golden and center is firm to the touch, about 1 hour and 20 minutes.

Makes 1 loaf.

Irish Soda Scones

13½ ounces (3 cups less 5 tablespoons) all-purpose flour
   Pinch of salt
½ teaspoon baking soda
2 teaspoons baking powder
3 ounces (½ cup) sugar
1 tablespoon caraway seeds
2 large eggs, lightly beaten
8 ounces (1 cup) sour cream
⅓ cup raisins

Preheat the oven to 325° F. Lightly grease and flour a baking sheet and set aside. Combine all ingredients in a large bowl and mix well. Using a large serving spoon, drop batter by spoonfuls onto the prepared sheet. Bake until a toothpick inserted in the center comes out clean, about 25 minutes.

Makes about 20 scones.

Summer

Summer is blue skies, bird songs, bees, crickets in the grass, hummingbirds feeding in the impatiens—bliss.

S U M M E R

The mornings are cool and the grass is always wet; it feels so good on bare feet. Walking up the mountain with the dogs before the day begins, past the pond so quiet, it's just us. The dogs travel all in a row through the tall grass not yet cut. We follow until we get to the woods and then they're off. We continue on up and up, looking back across the meadows to the hills beyond the valley, then more and more hills right into New York State—mountaintop after mountaintop!

By mid-summer everything is alive with beauty. The hydrangeas, the bluebells, sweet William, peonies. The hosta grow in more places than they did the year before, and the impatiens—pink, fuchsia, white, and red—crowd around the tree in the barnyard. The herbs are thick in the garden. The red farm wagon gets older each year, fading steadily. After years of work, it now sits still, full of blooming impatiens, looking content amid the thriving herbs. A few feet away, the cats peer out from the stone floor of the old milkhouse. They watch us watching them and the new kittens. (There are always new kittens in summer.) The sunflowers are tall and strong, soon full of seeds to feed the birds. They usually grow in one spot, but sometimes a few get away; one strayed into the barnyard, two into the vegetable garden, and two more out front along the road.

The pleasures of summer are different for us all. Skitch starts up the tractor and takes it to task in the pasture. The children swim and swim. Ruth waters the garden in her bare feet, or harvests tomatoes, or fills a basket with fresh-cut snapdragons and zinnias. But for everybody, there's no pleasure like sharing a meal with good friends by the pond, then cutting into a ripe watermelon for dessert and spitting the seeds into the water.

PRECEDING PAGES: *All the fences on the farm have mellowed with age. We tend them carefully so they will last a long, long time.* ABOVE: *The Mini Moke is Ruth's constant summertime sidekick. Since Skitch gave it to her, more than twenty years ago, it has spent the hot months running errands, transporting children, dogs, baskets of flowers . . .*

TOP: *Before coming to shore, Isabelle will always dive to the bottom to retrieve a stick or stone.* CENTER: *Long ago, we bought a small farm in Vermont and the 1930s tractor came with the deal.* ABOVE: *It's always a delicious surprise to look out from the 1836 Barn and see the cows at the gate.* RIGHT: *Glorious antique roses bloom in front of the twin silos.*

Summer

Fourth of July Picnic

•

*Summer Soups and
Salads*

•

*Hot-Day Drinks with
Sweets and Savories*

•

Ah! The Beloved Lobster

•

*Certainly Summer
Desserts*

•

The Firemen's Lunch

LEFT: *The time to restore the Chevy pick-up has not yet come. It sits undisturbed in the quiet of the pasture all summer long.* ABOVE: *We will hop in the Mini Moke or the jeep and head for the nearby peach orchard many times before summer is over.*

Summer

147

Fourth of July Picnic

*A*lmost every year we picnic with sixty or seventy friends and neighbors in a meadow owned by our friends Leo Altschul and Paul Lammers. Each family sets up its own picnic, so we choose a meal that travels well. This one, complete with serving platters, place settings, and folding table, fits entirely in Ruth's mother's laundry cart. Six Hendersons have plenty to eat with this menu, and there's extra for wandering friends who visit and taste from our table. That, in fact, is how we all pass the time out there in the meadow as we wait for darkness—meandering from picnic to picnic, talking, tasting, raising a ruckus. Only when the fireworks begin to explode above the town of Washington in the valley below do we settle down for the show.

Last year we picnicked in our barnyard to celebrate the homecoming of our son, Hans, his wife, Sandra, and our grandchildren Keiran and Kythera. The meal travels well. Even if it's only from kitchen to barnyard, we like things to be as easy as possible.

Smoked Turkey with Spiced Crabapples and Onions

○

Thirteen-Bean and Sausage Salad

○

Deviled Eggs

○

Fresh Berries in White Chocolate Cups

FAR LEFT: *A bed of brilliant impatiens grows around the shade tree in The Silo barnyard. It has become almost as well known as The Silo Christmas tree.* LEFT: *The table setting is red, white, and blue for the holiday. Blueberries were picked close by at the berry farm on Baldwin Hill.* ABOVE: *We can't resist letting the vines have their way on the silo. In the fall, however, we cut them away and plug any holes.*

Next-Day Smoked Turkey

Here at the farm, it's traditional for breakfast the day after any turkey dinner to serve a slice of turkey with two eggs sunny-side up. Skitch loves the white meat. Ruth's choice is the dark. We're a perfect turkey couple.

Also, the turkey carcass can be used to make a very rich, smoky stock in which to cook pasta, beans, or rice. It makes a hearty gravy and a terrific aspic.

Or you could purée 1 cup shredded leftover turkey, ¼ cup mayonnaise, 4 black olives, and a pinch of sage in a food processor until smooth. This makes a wonderful spread for flatbreads and crackers.

RIGHT: *The smoked turkey came from Virginia by mail order. Cured and smoked meats and fish are ideal for summer entertaining—the taste is superb hot or cold. The meal is served in the barnyard herb garden, and the smells of sage, marjoram, dill, lovage, and rosemary enhance the flavors of the food. A folk art Lady Liberty blesses the scene.* FAR RIGHT: *We used the leaves from tall stalks of lovage to garnish the bean salad, a good complement to the flavor of balsamic vinegar in the dressing.*

Smoked Turkey with Spiced Crabapples and Onions

Purchase your smoked turkey from a reliable source or, if you are one of the growing numbers of people who are using smokers, smoke it yourself. Cooking with Fire and Smoke *by Phillip Stephen Schulz (Simon and Schuster, 1986) is an excellent guide for the amateur smoker.*

  1 smoked turkey, about 15 pounds
  4 red onions, peeled and thinly sliced
10 spiced crabapples, at room temperature

Preheat the oven to 300° F. Place turkey on a rack in a roasting pan and roast until heated through, about 1½ hours. Arrange onion slices to cover a large serving platter. Place turkey on platter and fill opening of cavity with crabapples.

Serves 6, with enough leftovers for another meal.

Thirteen-Bean and Sausage Salad

This must be made the day before so it can marinate overnight.

- 1   24-ounce package Silo Thirteen-Bean Mix (or make your own dried bean mix from white beans, red beans, navy beans, and red and yellow lentils)
- 1   16-ounce package dried red beans
- 8   black peppercorns
- 1   sprig fresh marjoram
- 2   bay leaves
- ½   pound (about 8 links) breakfast sausage, cut into ½-inch lengths
- ½   teaspoon salt
- 2   teaspoons Dijon-style mustard
    Juice of ½ lemon
- ¾   cup olive oil
- 2½ tablespoons balsamic vinegar
- 2   tablespoons caraway seeds, lightly crushed with mortar and pestle
- ½   teaspoon freshly ground black pepper

Wash the beans and drain in a colander. In 2 large bowls, cover the mixed beans with water and, separately, cover the red beans with water and soak overnight; discard any beans that float. Place both varieties of beans and the soaking water all together in a large saucepan. Add more water if needed to cover. Make a bouquet garni of the peppercorns, marjoram, and bay leaves by tying them in a piece of cheesecloth with string and add to beans. Heat to boiling, reduce heat, and simmer until beans are just tender but still firm, about 1 hour. Drain. Discard bouquet garni.

Meanwhile, in a medium skillet over medium-high heat, cook the sausage until brown; drain on paper towels.

Combine the beans and sausage in a large salad or serving bowl. In a small bowl, combine the salt and mustard. Whisk in the lemon juice, oil, vinegar, caraway seeds, and pepper. Add to bean mixture while it is still warm; toss until well coated. Cover and refrigerate overnight.

Serves 6, with lots left over for other meals.

Next-Day Meals

Combine two cups shredded leftover turkey and any leftover beans from the Thirteen-Bean Salad in a soup pot. Cover with water or turkey stock. Heat to boiling, reduce heat, and simmer until warmed through.

Alternatively, you could purée the leftover beans in a food processor until smooth, adding water or stock if necessary. This is wonderful served with beef, pork, or sausage.

Or, if you prefer, make a purée as above, then transfer it to a saucepan. Add enough water or stock to make a smooth soup. Heat to boiling, reduce heat, and simmer five minutes. Ladle into soup bowls and garnish with chopped parsley.

Deviled Eggs

Hard-boiled eggs are a traditional picnic dish. For something fancier than what we did here, garnish with caviar, capers, a dash of paprika, or a slice of olive.

> 1 dozen large hard-boiled eggs, peeled
> 1 tablespoon prepared horseradish
> ½ cup mayonnaise
> 2 tablespoons Dijon-style mustard
> Salt and freshly ground black pepper

Cut eggs in half lengthwise. Scoop out yolks and place in a medium bowl. Place whites on a serving platter.

Add horseradish, mayonnaise, and mustard to egg yolks; stir until well blended. Add salt and pepper to taste. Using a small spoon, fill each egg white with the egg-yolk mixture. Serve immediately or refrigerate until ready to serve.

Makes 24 stuffed eggs.

Fresh Berries
in White Chocolate Cups

Ruedi Hauser, the chocolatier, has taught here at The Silo many times. His chocolate cups are very easy to make, and they're perfect for a variety of dessert fillings. All you'll need to buy are the dessert molds from a gourmet store or catalog. You can also find the cups ready-made in some fine food shops.

For this patriotic dessert, fill each white chocolate cup with the red and blue berries. We usually don't need to add anything to sweeten the berries. If you want extra sweetener, make a glaze by heating ½ cup of your favorite fruit jelly until it liquefies. Cool slightly and drizzle over the berries. Ruedi's recipe makes twenty-four chocolate cups. You can store any extras in a cool place.

> 1½ pounds white chocolate
> 1 pint fresh raspberries, washed
> 1 pint fresh blueberries, washed

To make the dessert cups, grate the chocolate and place two-thirds of it in the top of a double boiler over simmering water (the bottom of the pan should not be touching water). Stir constantly until chocolate is melted and

LEFT: *It's the berries and it's the chocolate, too! Ruedi Hauser sells these chocolate cups in attractive silver boxes. In a pinch, call The Silo and we'll send you some. They come in dark chocolate, too.*

temperature reads 110° F. on a candy thermometer. Remove the top of the double boiler and set it on a towel. Add remaining chocolate, stirring until completely melted and temperature cools to 75° F. Set back on top of boiler. Reheat over simmering water, stirring constantly, until temperature reads 89° F. (91° F. when using dark chocolate).

Wipe the insides of 24 2-ounce (¼-cup) dessert molds with soft cotton. Fill each with chocolate. Let stand 4 minutes, then invert on a rack placed over a baking sheet. Excess chocolate will drain down to baking sheet. (This excess chocolate can be saved for use in another recipe.) Scrape any excess from edges of the molds with a metal spatula. Allow 1 hour to set, then unmold and store in a cool place.

Fill 6 of the cooled cups with raspberries and blueberries.

Serves 6.

OPPOSITE, TOP: *Red bee balm, which provides feasts for humming-birds, has taken over one corner of the herb garden. We will divide it next spring and find an additional spot for it to grow.*
OPPOSITE, CENTER: *White daisies are everywhere! Kythera makes garlands, Ruth ties napkins with them, and Skitch puts them in the buttonhole of his blue-jean jacket.*
OPPOSITE, BOTTOM: *Bluebells grow in one-sided clusters. One tall stem, with buds, open bells, and leaves, will look like a work of art when placed in a narrow vase or bottle.*

Summer Soups
and Salads

For several years, Ruth and her invaluable executive right-hand woman, Eileen FitzGerald, planned and created the gardens that thrive now in several locations all over the farm. Orange lilies grow thick along the driveway, impatiens thrive in beds under trees and around corners, and another collection of lilies grows in front of the stone wall near the 1836 Barn. There's the cutting garden, an ample herb garden next to the old milkhouse, and a huge vegetable garden that we all "root" for each summer. Our daughter-in-law, Sandra, spent her first months here tending the vegetables with love and sweat. In fact, it seems that many who have lived here have contributed to the gardens and the beauty of the farm. Our first partner, Louise King, made a gift to us of the antique roses that grow in front of The Silo. Thanks to everybody who has planted, hoed, and weeded, the grounds are now lush and beautiful and we have an abundant supply of herbs, berries, flowers, and vegetables all summer long.

We usually like to make these soups from our first harvest of vegetables each summer. We serve them well chilled on a very hot day. The salads are light, whole meals in themselves, which we toss just before serving.

Curried Squash Bisque

○

Summer Squash Cream

○

Very Cool Cucumber Soup

○

Provolone Salad with Red-Basil Vinaigrette

○

Salad of Romaine, Fresh Lovage, and Spicy Beef with Thyme Vinaigrette

○

Boston Greens and Cajun Ham with Dill Vinaigrette

FAR LEFT: *Our gardens usually produce lots of vegetables, herbs, and flowers. When there's an overabundance, we set up a table and umbrella in front of The Silo and sell our surplus. Cold soups made from garden overflow are ideal eating during a heat wave. Refrigerate and frost a glass serving bowl and individual soup bowls and the meal will refresh the eye as well as the palate.*
LEFT: *This wild rose was introduced to Litchfield County years ago as a means of erosion control. Since then, it has taken off and taken over valuable pasture land. Now, the wild rose must be tamed.*

ABOVE: *One lone orange lily has found its way to the pink, salmon, and red impatiens bed. Nature has its own way of painting colors.*
BELOW: *When Hans was a teenager, his summer job with the highway department put him in the right place at the right time. Hundreds of lilies were discarded as the workers widened the road. He brought them home and here they live!*

Curried Squash Bisque

2 tablespoons (¼ stick) unsalted butter
2 onions, finely chopped
6 yellow summer squash (about 2 pounds), trimmed and thinly sliced
Juice of 1 lemon
½ teaspoon ground cumin
½ teaspoon ground coriander
2 teaspoons mustard seeds
½ teaspoon turmeric
2 cups chicken stock
1 teaspoon freshly ground black pepper
Salt

Melt the butter in a large saucepan over medium-low heat. Add the onions and cook until soft, about 5 minutes. Add squash, lemon juice, cumin, coriander, mustard seeds, turmeric, chicken stock, and pepper. Heat to boiling; reduce heat and simmer, covered, until the squash is tender, about 8 to 10 minutes. Cool.

Place mixture in a food processor or blender and process until smooth. Add salt to taste. Refrigerate and serve well chilled.

Serves 6–8.

Summer Squash Cream

6 yellow summer squash or zucchini (about 2 pounds), trimmed and thinly sliced
2 tablespoons (¼ stick) unsalted butter
2 onions, finely chopped
½ cup finely chopped fresh basil
¼ teaspoon salt
¼ teaspoon freshly ground black pepper
½ cup sour cream or yogurt
Approximately 2 cups milk

Place the squash in a vegetable steamer. Heat water to boiling, cover, and steam until tender, about 5–8 minutes.

Melt the butter in a skillet over medium heat. Add the onions and cook until soft, about 5 minutes. Add the squash to the skillet; toss to coat with the onion mixture. Cool.

Place onions and squash in a food processor and process until smooth. Add the basil, salt, pepper, and sour cream. Process again until well blended. With processor on, slowly add the milk until mixture reaches the desired consistency. Refrigerate and serve well chilled.

Serves 6.

Summer Soups and Salads

TOP: *Isabelle, playing it cool, waits for Ruth to throw a stone.* ABOVE: *Sheba wades in to cool her feet only every once in a while. That's as far as she'll go.*

Very Cool Cucumber Soup

8 tablespoons (1 stick) unsalted butter
2 onions, finely chopped (1½ cups)
¼ cup all-purpose flour
3 cucumbers, peeled, seeded, and cubed (5 cups)
5 cups chicken stock
  Salt and freshly ground black pepper
1 cup half and half

Melt the butter in a large saucepan over medium heat. Add the onions and cook until soft, about 5 minutes. Gradually add the flour, stirring constantly until thick. Add the cucumbers, chicken stock, and salt and pepper to taste. Heat to boiling; reduce heat and simmer 25 minutes. Cool.

  Pour soup into a food processor or blender and process until smooth. Chill 3 hours. Two hours before serving, add the half and half, stirring until well blended. Serve well chilled.

  Serves 6–8.

Provolone Salad with Red-Basil Vinaigrette

When salad is the main course, give it the spotlight. Use the freshest ingredients, along with special oils and vinegars. Display the makings for two or three different salads and let guests watch you combine and toss. They love it. And it makes the hostess look terrific!

1 head red oak-leaf lettuce, separated into leaves
1 head green leaf lettuce, separated into leaves
1 scallion, chopped (¼ cup)
½ cup cured black olives
¼ pound provolone cheese, cut into 2 × ¼-inch strips
3 sprigs fresh marjoram, chopped, or 1 tablespoon dried
¼ teaspoon Dijon-style mustard
2 tablespoons red-basil vinegar*
  Salt and freshly ground white pepper
½ cup Greek olive oil

Wash the lettuce leaves and pat dry. Line a salad bowl with the red leaves. Arrange the green leaves in the center. Place the scallion, olives, and cheese around the center of green leaves. Sprinkle with the marjoram.

To make the vinaigrette, combine the mustard, vinegar, salt, and pepper to taste in a small bowl. Whisk in the oil. Toss the salad with the dressing just before serving.

Serves 6.

*Red-basil vinegar is available in most fine food shops.

Salad of Romaine, Fresh Lovage, and Spicy Beef with Thyme Vinaigrette

This whole-meal salad can be made with any meat. We prepare the steak the day before so it can marinate overnight. It imparts a very special taste to the salad.

- 1 pound boneless beef sirloin, 1 to 1½ inches thick
- 2 tablespoons Cajun blackening spice
  Vegetable oil
- 1 large onion (preferably Vidalia), thinly sliced
- 1 clove garlic, peeled and mashed
- ½ teaspoon salt
- 1 teaspoon mustard (we prefer a beer mustard for this)
  Juice of ½ lemon
- ¾ cup vegetable oil
- 1 tablespoon red-wine vinegar
- 1 large head Romaine lettuce, leaves separated
- ¼ cup chopped fresh sage
- 4 leaves fresh lovage, chopped
- 2 tablespoons thyme vinegar
- ¼ teaspoon freshly ground pepper from red peppercorns
- ½ cup French olive oil

The day before serving, sprinkle each side of the sirloin with 1 tablespoon of the blackening spice and press it into the meat with the heel of your palm. Let stand 10 minutes.

Heat only enough vegetable oil to coat a large skillet until hot but not smoking. Cook the steak until it reaches the desired doneness—about 5 minutes on each side for rare. Remove meat to a cutting board and allow to cool slightly. Meanwhile, add the onion to the skillet and sauté just until

RIGHT: *Our supper of salads is prepared and tossed at the stone table near the pool house. The top was found at the nearby Roxbury quarry. Because it weighs 1,500 pounds, it's a permanent fixture.*

BELOW: *Each salad is spiced with a different pepper. We used freshly ground green peppercorns on this ham salad.*

soft, about 5 minutes. Cut the steak into ¼-inch-thick slices and place in a ceramic or glass dish. Place the onion on top of the beef.

Mash the garlic with the salt in a small bowl until it is the consistency of a paste. Add the mustard and lemon juice. Whisk in the oil and vinegar. Pour over the beef and onion. Cover and refrigerate overnight.

Just before serving, allow steak and onion to come to room temperature. Arrange on a serving platter.

To make the salad, wash the lettuce leaves, pat dry, tear into the desired size, and place in a salad bowl. Sprinkle with sage and lovage.

To make the vinaigrette, combine vinegar and pepper in a small bowl. Whisk in the oil. Toss the salad with the dressing. Serve with the beef and onion on the side. (Of course, you can choose to cut the beef into 1-inch-long strips, chop the onion, and toss with the salad. It's delicious either way.)

Serves 6–8.

Boston Greens and Cajun Ham with Dill Vinaigrette

Here is another salad we prefer to serve with the meat alongside. The ham looks terrific on its own platter.

> 1 pre-cooked ham steak, about 1 pound
> 1 tablespoon Cajun blackening spice
>   Vegetable oil
> 1 head Boston lettuce, leaves separated
> 6 cherry tomatoes, halved
> ¼ cup chopped chives
> 3 large leaves fresh red basil, chopped, plus several extra
>   leaves for garnish
> 2 tablespoons dill vinegar
> ¼ teaspoon freshly ground pepper from green peppercorns
> ½ cup sunflower oil

Sprinkle both sides of the ham steak with the blackening spice and press it into the meat with the heel of your palm. Let stand 10 minutes. Heat just enough vegetable oil to coat a medium skillet until hot but not smoking. Add the ham and cook 5 minutes per side. Cool and slice in ¼-inch-thick strips and place on a serving plate.

Wash the lettuce, pat dry, tear the leaves into pieces of the desired size, and place them in a salad bowl. Place the tomatoes in the center. Sprinkle the salad with the chives and chopped basil.

To make the vinaigrette, combine the vinegar and pepper in a small bowl. Whisk in the oil. Toss the salad with the dressing and garnish with basil leaves.

Serves 4–6.

TOP: *The Vermont wooden bowl holds a true Henderson house salad for hungry company. We combine ingredients from all three salads in this chapter, add sliced radish and hard-boiled eggs, and toss with red basil vinaigrette.* ABOVE: *We once dismantled this wall to rescue a litter of kittens. We had allowed mother and kittens privacy, and we didn't miss them until we heard their cries. Kittens and wall survived.*

Summer Soups and Salads

Hot-Day Drinks with Sweets and Savories

We have many friends and neighbors who come by on a summer day to shop at The Silo Store and say hello. These liquid refreshers are easy to stir up for them at the last minute. For occasions when there's time to plan, we serve these savories and sweets, too.

Lemon Beer

∘

Bloody Pilgrim

∘

Red-Ice Lemon Cooler

∘

Puff Cheesesticks

∘

Savory Herb Biscuits

∘

Oatmeal Chunk Cookies

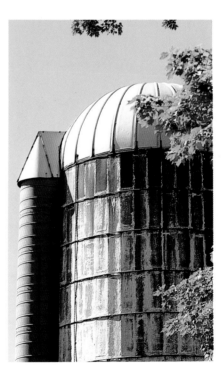

LEFT: *The texture, color, and thickness of our Mexican and Spanish glassware suit our indoor-outdoor life.* ABOVE: *The red rocker on the deck off Ruth's office sits empty too often. Here, it awaits a daydreamer.* RIGHT: *We've experimented with uses for our one and only stone silo. It's not a good wine cellar, but it does store apples and potatoes in warm months and firewood in winter.*

Lemon Beer

    Ice cubes
3 12-ounce containers cold light beer
    Juice of 1 lemon
¼ cup superfine sugar
1 lemon, thinly sliced

Place 6 ice cubes in a chilled 2- to 2½-quart pitcher. Add one container of beer by pouring slowly down the side of the tilted pitcher. Stir in lemon juice and sugar. When foam subsides a little, add remaining beer and half the lemon slices and stir gently.

    Fill 4 glasses half full with ice. Add a lemon slice to each and fill with the lemon beer.

    Serves 4.

Bloody Pilgrim

    Ice cubes
    Juice of 1 lime
10 ounces (1¼ cups) vodka, or more or less to taste
    Cranberry juice, chilled
1 lime, sliced

Fill a chilled 2- to 2½-quart pitcher one-quarter full with ice. Add lime juice, vodka, and enough cranberry juice to fill; stir well. Serve with more ice and a slice of lime in each glass. Make a Virgin Pilgrim by eliminating the vodka.

    Serves 4.

Red-Ice Lemon Cooler

This is a fancy version of a drink we have available in the refrigerator all summer long. Plain old lemon in water is one of the most welcomed refreshers anybody hot and dry ever sipped. We consume pitchers and pitchers of it.

    8 ounces (1 cup) cassis (black currant syrup)
    ½ cup water
    1 lemon, sliced, plus extra for garnish

T O P : *The tobacco barn was re-sided in 1979 with rough pine. Inside, stained-glass windows from Daly's, illuminated by electric light, along with café tables and garden chairs, can create a refuge from a rained-out barbecue.* A B O V E : *The garden chairs line up in The Silo barnyard for a midsummer barbecue class.*

Summer

To make the red ice, mix the cassis and water in a small pitcher or bowl. Pour into two 12-cube ice trays (we used heart-shaped cube trays) and place in freezer overnight. Fill a 2-quart pitcher with water and lemon slices and refrigerate overnight.

Just before serving, place a few red ice cubes in each of 4 chilled glasses. Add remaining ice cubes to the pitcher and fill glasses with the lemon water and garnish with extra lemon slices.

Serves 4.

Puff Cheesesticks

These are rich and addictive. They also keep frozen very well—up to six months.

1¼ pounds (4 cups) all-purpose flour
1¼ pounds (5 sticks) unsalted butter, cut into small bits
1 cup water
1 tablespoon salt
8 ounces (about 2 cups) cheddar cheese, finely grated

Combine the flour and butter in a large bowl. Using 2 knives or a pastry blender, cut in the butter until mixture is the texture of coarse bread crumbs. Add the water and salt and mix until a soft dough forms. Form into a ball, wrap in wax paper, and chill 1 hour.

Preheat the oven to 400° F. Lightly grease a baking sheet and set aside. Lightly flour a smooth surface and sprinkle with the cheese. Roll out the chilled pastry on this surface to form a square, about ¼ inch thick. Cut into strips about 6–8 inches long and ½ inch wide. Twist each strip into a spiral and place on prepared baking sheet. Bake until puffed and golden, about 10 minutes. Cool on a rack.

Makes about 100 cheesesticks.

ABOVE: *We call this* Sommerbier *in Germany, where it is served in* Gartenrestaurants.

ABOVE: *Mexican glass turtles, with holes just big enough for a hand, keep summer insects at bay. They hold, from left, herb biscuits, oatmeal cookies, and cheesesticks.*

Savory Herb Biscuits

1¼ pounds (4 cups) all-purpose flour
1¼ pounds (5 sticks) unsalted butter
½ cup water
⅓ ounce (2 teaspoons) salt
2 ounces (½ cup less 1 tablespoon) flour
1 bunch chives, chopped
1 tablespoon freshly ground black pepper
1 teaspoon garlic salt

Combine 4 cups flour and butter in a large bowl. Using 2 knives or a pastry blender, cut in the butter until mixture is the texture of coarse bread crumbs. Add the water and salt and mix until a soft dough forms. Form into a ball, wrap in wax paper, and chill 1 hour.

Preheat the oven to 400° F. Lightly grease a baking sheet and set aside.

Combine the 2 ounces flour, chives, pepper, and garlic salt in a small bowl. Sprinkle this mixture on a smooth surface. Roll out the chilled dough on this prepared surface to form a square about ¼ inch thick. Cut into 2-inch rounds with a biscuit or cookie cutter. Place biscuits on prepared baking sheet. Bake until golden, about 10 minutes. Cool on a rack.

Makes about 3 dozen biscuits.

Oatmeal Chunk Cookies

    8 tablespoons (1 stick) unsalted butter, softened
    2½ ounces (5 tablespoons) granulated sugar
    2½ ounces (⅓ cup) light brown sugar, firmly packed
    2 large eggs, slightly beaten
    1 teaspoon vanilla extract
    3 ounces (1 cup) rolled oats
    5 ounces (1 cup) all-purpose flour
      Pinch of salt
    1 teaspoon baking soda
    3 ounces (⅔ cup) raisins
    1 teaspoon ground cinnamon
    3 ounces (¾ cup, plus 2 tablespoons) pecans, roughly
      chopped
    3 ounces (½ cup) chocolate chips

Preheat the oven to 350° F. Lightly grease a baking sheet and set aside. Beat the butter and sugars together in a mixing bowl until light yellow in color. Beat in the eggs and vanilla. Add the remaining ingredients one at a time, beating well after each addition. Drop by rounded teaspoonfuls onto the prepared sheet. Bake until pale brown and firm to the touch, about 12–15 minutes. Cool on a rack.

Makes 36 cookies.

TOP: *A giant peony from our garden is heavy after a rain. Several varieties also appear near the Main House and Hunt Hill Cottage—evidence of a green thumb at work long before ours.* ABOVE: *The Bloody Pilgrim has been served in the Henderson house since the summers we spent in Long Pond, Massachusetts, where we were surrounded by cranberry bogs.*

Ah! The Beloved Lobster

There is nothing more summer, nor more New England, than fresh lobster enjoyed in the company of friends. Ruth didn't taste her first lobster until she was twenty-one, refusing all seafood until then. What a waste! But she's certainly made up for it since! Hot days here by the pond, the brook, the pool—wherever the water flows—provide irresistible occasions for cooking up fresh lobster. Here are two feasts—the little and the big of it!

Lobster at Poolside

◦

Lime Sorbet

◦

The Clambake

LEFT: *The lobsters sit on platters made from construction glass by Priscilla Porter, a local craftswoman. They can be heated or chilled without sustaining any damage.* ABOVE: *Our Hunt Hill clambake is fast, efficient, and foolproof. The pond is not exactly the New England seacoast, but it suits us and our guests just fine.* RIGHT: *Wilton Armetale makes dinnerware that answers Ruth's needs, especially on clambake day—it's handsome, unbreakable, and oversized, and it looks great alongside pewter, copper, pottery, and wood.*

Lobster at Poolside

One day Skitch brought two of his colleagues from the New York Pops up to the farm to do some work. But it was so hot that they spent most of their time cooling off in the pool! For an early supper, Ruth surprised everyone with these platters.

  8 small red potatoes
     Salt
  4 lobsters, about 1½ pounds each
12 scallions, trimmed
  8 tablespoons (1 stick) unsalted butter, clarified
  1 lemon, cut in wedges

Cook the potatoes in boiling salted water until tender, about 15 minutes. Drain.

Meanwhile, immerse the lobsters, head first, in a large pot of boiling salted water. Allow water to return to a boil, reduce heat, and simmer 12 minutes. Drain. Crack the claws of each lobster and cut down the length of the underside with a sharp knife. (This makes it easier for your diners to get started.) Hold each lobster up by its claws so it drains of excess water before placing it on a platter with the potatoes, scallions, a small cup of the clarified butter, and a lemon wedge.

Serves 4.

ABOVE: *Hosta is always plentiful around the pool, but when it blooms it is a spectacular sight.*

FAR LEFT: *On very hot days, we really love to stand in the pool and reach for the lobsters sitting on the stone deck. Not great manners, but no one has ever complained.*

Lime Sorbet

We try to have frozen desserts like this sorbet on hand in the freezer all summer long. You can freeze this either in a large bowl or in individual serving glasses.

     Juice of 18 fresh limes (about 2 cups)
  2 cups sugar
     Zest of 4 limes
1½ cups heavy cream
 ½ cup water
  1 lime, thinly sliced

Place all ingredients except lime slices in a food processor and process until smooth. Place mixture in an ice cream maker and freeze according to manufacturer's instructions. Spoon into a 1-quart soufflé dish and serve immediately, or place in freezer until ready to serve. Remove from freezer 20 minutes before serving and garnish with slices of fresh lime.

Makes 1 quart.

BELOW: *We enjoy tangy lime or lemon desserts after seafood.*

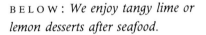

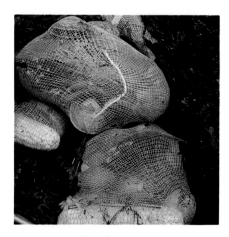

ABOVE: *These bags came from our fish market; cheesecloth can also be cut and tied with twine to hold the meal while boiling.*

The Clambake

All you need is an outdoor gas burner, a large washtub, a picnic table, and people. If you don't have an outdoor burner, you can rent one or boil your catch indoors and serve it outside. But we feel that outdoors, and preferably near water, is the best place for this event. At our table, we encourage everyone to enjoy each bite using his or her hands. Each guest has a king-size napkin, which actually is a towel, and total freedom to make the mess that goes with a good clambake. There are two or three large finger bowls or individual bowls filled with water and fresh lemon slices.

Adjust this recipe up or down according to your desired guest list. You will want to purchase cheesecloth poaching bags from your fish merchant and seaweed from the same source. Enjoy!

> 12 lobsters, about 1½ pounds each
> 24 small red potatoes
> 12 small onions
> 48 mussels, scrubbed and beards removed
> 48 littleneck clams, rinsed well
> 12 sprigs fresh dill
> 12 small to medium ears fresh corn, shucked
> 2 pounds seaweed
> 1½ pounds (6 sticks) unsalted butter, clarified
> 6 lemons

Place 1 lobster, 2 potatoes, 1 onion, 4 mussels, 4 clams, 1 sprig of dill, and 1 ear of corn in each of 12 cheesecloth poaching bags and tie each bag tightly. (If you can't find poaching bags, tie the corners of a large sheet of cheesecloth together with string or twine to form a sack.)

Heat a large pot or washtub filled with water to boiling. Add as many filled poaching bags as possible, top with the seaweed, and cover tightly. (At our clambake, where we used a washtub, we had to improvise a cover of aluminum foil.) When water returns to a boil, reduce heat and simmer 10 minutes. Remove bags with tongs and drain. (You now have a stock that is well worth saving.)

Remove the shellfish and vegetables from each bag and arrange on each guest's plate. Or, place everything in a large bowl in the center of the table and let guests reach and fill their own plates. Serve with individual cups of melted clarified butter, lemon slices, and extra butter for the corn.

Serves 12.

A B O V E : *Heidi is the notorious champion in the family when it comes to devouring lobster. She goes at it with such enthusiasm that, when she's finished, even the cats can't find a smidgen of meat left!*

Ah! The Beloved Lobster

Certainly Summer Desserts

*B*erries and fruits grow in great abundance here. We have served these desserts both formally and informally to our friends and guests.

Berry Mary Anns

o

Ice Cream Berry Shake

o

Cool Fruit Mousses

o

Melon Mélanges

o

Whole-Fruit Compote for a Crowd

LEFT: *Sometimes it's interesting to do things in threes—everyone has a choice. Here, three monkeys hold, from top, melon mélanges, berry shakes, and fruit mousses.* ABOVE: *An old tree stump holding the cakes has been in service in The Silo barnyard for a long time. The pain of having to cut down old trees is eased a little when we can keep and use the stumps.* RIGHT: *For a quick snack, eat these melon balls right from the jar. Refrigerated, they will stay very firm and need nothing more than a squeeze of lemon juice.*

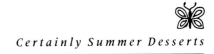

Old-fashioned stirred puddings rather than fancier pastry creams constitute the fillings for each of these Mary Anns. Ruth likes the gentle, constant stirring and the homey, substantial taste. The first thing Ruth ever fixed Skitch to eat was a chocolate pudding. He came to visit at her little apartment on Jane Street in New York in the afternoon, and she had very little time to make something for him to eat. So she made the pudding; it was still warm when he ate it. And one would have thought he'd been given a million dollars.

The important thing to remember about making pudding is to use a heavy pan to avoid scorching and, of course, to keep stirring. Yes, a pudding made from one of the packaged mixes will do in a pinch. If you do use a mix, cook it according to the instructions on the box. As the pudding cools, add a splash of liqueur and some nuts or raisins, as we have suggested.

Any leftover pudding can be put in dessert cups, covered with plastic wrap, chilled, and enjoyed with whipped cream.

Berry Mary Anns

Basic Cake

We like to make two of these at a time, wrap the extra one in plastic, and keep it in the freezer. To have the cake ready-made lets you prepare these wonderful Mary Anns on very short notice.

- 8 tablespoons (1 stick) unsalted butter, softened
- 5 ounces (¾ cup) granulated sugar
  Pinch of salt
- 2 large eggs, separated
  Grated zest of ½ lemon
- ¼ teaspoon almond extract
- 2 teaspoons dark rum
- ⅛ teaspoon cream of tartar
- 4 ounces (1 cup less 3 tablespoons) all-purpose flour

Preheat the oven to 350° F. Butter and flour a 9-inch flan or Mary Ann mold and set aside.

Beat the butter, 4 ounces of the sugar, and the salt together in a mixing bowl until smooth. Beat in the egg yolks one at a time. Add the lemon zest, almond extract, and rum; beat until well blended.

In another bowl, beat the egg whites with the cream of tartar until soft peaks form. Add remaining 1 ounce of sugar and continue beating until egg whites are stiff but not dry.

Fold egg whites and flour alternately into the butter-egg mixture. Spoon batter into the prepared pan and bake until a toothpick inserted in the center comes out clean, about 30 minutes. Cool on wire rack. Unmold.

Makes one 9-inch cake.

Strawberry-Blueberry Mary Ann

- 3 tablespoons raisins
- ¼ cup light rum
- 1 large egg
- ½ cup sugar
- 2 tablespoons cornstarch
- 2 cups milk
- 1 teaspoon vanilla extract
- 1 tablespoon unsalted butter, softened
- 1 basic Mary Ann cake (see recipe, page 176)
- 1 pint fresh strawberries, washed and hulled
- 1 cup fresh blueberries, washed and picked over

Place the raisins in a small cup. Cover with rum and let soak overnight.

Beat the egg lightly in a small bowl and set aside. Heat the sugar and cornstarch in a heavy saucepan over medium heat. Gradually add the milk, stirring constantly. Heat to boiling and allow to boil 1 minute while continuing to stir. Reduce heat to *very* low and continue to stir and cook for 3 minutes. Add 2 tablespoons of the hot mixture to the egg and mix; return egg mixture to pan. Cook, stirring, 3 minutes longer. Do not boil. Remove from heat and add the vanilla, butter, and raisins; stir well. Cool slightly.

Place the cake bottom side up on a serving plate. Spread pudding inside the well in the center of the cake. Arrange strawberries and blueberries randomly on top of the pudding. Serve immediately or refrigerate until ready to serve.

Serves 8.

Blackberry or Raspberry Mary Ann

If you want to glaze any of these Mary Anns, heat ¼ cup of a good fruit jelly until it liquefies, and cool it slightly. Then drizzle it over the fruit. The Mary Ann will take on a sweet shine.

- 1 large egg
- ¾ cup dark brown sugar
- 2 tablespoons cornstarch
- 2 cups milk
- 1 teaspoon maple syrup
- 1 tablespoon unsalted butter
- 3 tablespoons Amaretto liqueur
- 3 tablespoons finely chopped walnuts
- 1 basic Mary Ann cake (see recipe, page 176)
- 2 pints fresh blackberries or raspberries, washed and picked over

Beat the egg lightly in a small bowl and set aside. Heat the brown sugar and cornstarch in a heavy saucepan over medium heat. Gradually add the milk, stirring constantly. Heat to boiling and allow to boil 1 minute while continuing to stir. Reduce heat to *very* low and continue to stir and cook 3 minutes. Add 2 tablespoons of the hot mixture to the egg and mix; return egg mixture to pan. Cook, stirring, 3 minutes longer. Do not boil. Remove from heat and stir in maple syrup, butter, liqueur, and walnuts. Cool slightly.

Place the cake bottom side up on a serving plate. Spread pudding inside the well in the center of the cake. Arrange blackberries randomly on top of the pudding. Serve immediately or refrigerate until ready to serve.

Serves 8.

TOP: *We like to go out in the morning and pick a handful of currants just to have them on cereal. They are also delicious with milk and a touch of sugar or yogurt.* ABOVE: *Use any berry or mixture of berries you like for the toppings on these desserts. We've also used whole-fruit preserves to top off the cake.*

Ice Cream Berry Shake

¾ cup vanilla ice cream
⅓ cup milk
1 cup fresh blackberries, raspberries, or strawberries, washed,
picked over, and hulled if necessary

Combine the ice cream, milk, and ½ cup berries in a blender; process until just blended, about 5 seconds. Reserve 5 of remaining berries for garnish, then add the rest to the ice cream mixture and stir gently with a spoon. Pour into a 12-ounce tulip glass. Garnish with the reserved berries and serve immediately.

Serves 1.

Cool Fruit Mousses

Sweet Peach Mousse

4 ripe peaches, peeled, pitted, and sliced
1¼ cups sugar
1½ tablespoons unflavored gelatin
½ cup orange juice
½ teaspoon almond extract
½ teaspoon freshly grated nutmeg
2 teaspoons grated orange zest
1½ cups sour cream
2 cups heavy cream
Fresh peach slices, for garnish

Purée the peaches in a food processor or blender until smooth. Combine the purée, sugar, and gelatin in a medium saucepan. Let stand 5 minutes. Heat over medium heat, stirring constantly, until gelatin dissolves, about 10 minutes. Remove from heat and allow to cool 20 minutes.

Add the orange juice, almond extract, nutmeg, and orange zest to the peach mixture; stir well. Whisk in the sour cream.

Beat the cream in a large bowl until soft peaks form. Fold peach mixture into cream. Spoon into dessert glasses or a 2-quart soufflé dish. Refrigerate several hours. Serve garnished with the fresh peach slices.

Serves 8–10.

Banana Mousse

- 3 ripe bananas, peeled and quartered
- ½ cup orange juice
- 1½ tablespoons unflavored gelatin
- ¼ cup cold water
- 1 tablespoon cornstarch
- 4 large eggs, separated
- 1 cup sugar
- ¼ cup Grand Marnier liqueur
- ½ teaspoon ground cinnamon, plus extra for garnish
- 1½ cups heavy cream
- Fresh mint and banana slices, for garnish

Purée the bananas with the orange juice in a food processor or blender until smooth. Combine the gelatin and water in a medium saucepan. Let stand 5 minutes. Add the banana mixture and cornstarch. Heat to boiling, then reduce heat. Cook, stirring constantly, over medium heat for 2 minutes. Remove from heat and allow to cool 20 minutes.

Beat the egg yolks and sugar in a bowl until light yellow in color. Add the liqueur and cinnamon and transfer to the top of a double boiler. Whisk over simmering water until mixture is hot to the touch. Stir in the banana mixture and allow to cool to room temperature.

Whip the cream until doubled in volume and very soft peaks have formed. Beat the egg whites until stiff but not dry. Fold the cream into the banana custard. Gently fold in egg whites. Spoon into a 2-quart soufflé dish or individual dessert glasses. Refrigerate several hours. Serve garnished with fresh mint and banana slices dusted with cinnamon.

Serves 8–10.

ABOVE: Of all the desserts we served, only the shakes had to be prepared and served immediately. Fresh berries garnish the top.

Melon Mélanges

These are highly spirited, for the grownups in your group.

Watermelon Mélange

- 1 large wedge watermelon (about 4 × 10 inches), seeds removed
- 2 ripe peaches, peeled, pitted, and sliced
- Juice of ½ lemon
- ¼ cup Triple Sec liqueur

OPPOSITE, TOP: Long before we ever thought we'd live on a farm, we bought and treasured this Belgian cow painting. OPPOSITE, BOTTOM: Life is a little sweeter when these ladies come visiting.

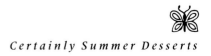

Cranshaw Mélange

½ large cranshaw melon, seeded and scraped
7 yellow plums, peeled and sliced, or 7 fresh apricots,
    washed, pitted, and quartered
Juice of ½ lemon
¼ cup Galliano liqueur

Honeydew Mélange

½ large honeydew melon, seeded and scraped
2 kiwifruit, sliced
Juice of 1 lime
¼ cup crème de menthe liqueur

Using a 1-inch melon baller, scoop 18 balls from the melon. Reserve 4 balls and refrigerate. Place the remaining 14 in a food processor or blender and process until smooth. Add the fresh fruit and process until smooth. Add the citrus juice and liqueur and process 10 seconds longer. Pour mixture into four 4-ounce glasses until each is three-fourths full. Place glasses in freezer until mixture is frozen, about 2 hours. Just before serving, garnish with the reserved melon balls.

Serves 4.

ABOVE: *We sip the spirits, then eat the rest of these mélanges with an English silver sipping spoon. If you have extra melon balls, they keep very well in the freezer for several weeks.*

Whole-Fruit Compote for a Crowd

Once, when we were expecting a big turnout for an opening in The Silo Gallery, we made this compote the day before, carried it out to the garden for a photograph, then served it the next day at the buffet for our opening-day guests. By then, the fruit had given off much of its natural juices. If you take the time to peel the fruit, the fruit does all the work. We added a little white wine. You can also add champagne, or a fruit syrup such as cassis.

3 dozen ripe peaches, peeled
1 cup fresh lemon juice
4½ dozen yellow plums, peeled
1 quart fresh gooseberries, washed and picked over
1 quart fresh bluberries, washed and picked over
2 pints fresh strawberries, washed, hulled, and picked over

2 pints fresh blackberries, washed and picked over
2 pints fresh raspberries, washed and picked over
    White wine (optional)

Layer the bottom of a 2-gallon wide-mouth jar with some of the peaches; sprinkle with ¼ cup of the lemon juice. Add a layer of yellow plums and sprinkle with another ¼ cup lemon juice. Add all the gooseberries, another layer of peaches, and another layer of plums; sprinkle with ¼ cup lemon juice. Add another layer of peaches; sprinkle with remaining lemon juice. Cover with strawberries, blackberries, and raspberries. Let stand 2 hours, then refrigerate 24 hours.

One hour before serving, remove from refrigerator. If compote has not filled the jar with its own fruit juices, add some white wine or champagne, liqueur, or a fruit syrup mixed with water to fill. Serve at room temperature.

Serves 50.

LEFT: *This is the best way we know to share all the fruits we love. The berries were picked here; nearby orchards supplied the rest.*

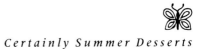

Certainly Summer Desserts

The Firemen's Lunch

We gave a lunch for a group of German firemen and their host families from the New Milford Water Witch Hose Company No. 2. By the time the guest list was completed, there were sixty people and our nearby Northville fire truck coming. We decided to seat everyone as well as park the truck in The Silo pasture. All hands got into this act. Our staff in the cooking school not only helped prepare the food but found themselves "volunteering" to paint sawhorses and set tables for the luncheon. Let there be no mistake: for this final feast of summer, we needed all the help we could get. And we'd do it again, probably hoping for a cooler-than-98-degree day, because the joy on the faces of our visitors when they bit into our New England version of a German lunch was priceless. *Ein Prosit!*

Our Best Wurst

o

Henderson Sauerkraut

o

Boiled New Potatoes

o

Dark Chocolate Brownies

FAR LEFT: *The Northville Volunteer Fire Department, a half mile away, saved us once from an unattended soup-pot fire that sent thick smoke billowing from the 1836 Barn. On the weekend when 80 Connecticut fire companies came to New Milford to celebrate the 125th birthday of the Water Witch Hose Company No. 2, the Northville volunteers were our guests for lunch.* LEFT: *We used planks from The Silo's old redwood deck and sawhorses to create a table big enough to seat 60 guests. It stretched across The Silo pasture.* ABOVE: *The visiting firefighters from Laupheim, West Germany, were the guests of honor. When the Bürgermeister broke into song, everyone joined in.* Prosit, ein Prosit der Gemütlichkeit!

TOP: *Alma did not miss one day of our cooking and photographing sessions for this book. She tasted everything—even the peaches. We lost her in the summer of 1989 and we miss her wherever we turn.* ABOVE: *The sauerkraut and the sausages are served in one bowl, so everything stays moist and warm. The spoonfork is ideal for serving both.*
ABOVE, RIGHT: *Plain boiled potatoes fill tin bowls and colanders hold the very fragile white peaches.*

Our Best Wurst

We planned on each German luncheoneer having three different wurst apiece, as is the custom. And we counted on each of our other guests having half of each wurst. Of course, purchase the wurst from a reliable butcher. Ours is Schaller and Weber.

    48 links bratwurst (pork)
       Vegetable oil
    48 links weisswurst (veal)
    48 links bauernwurst (smoked beef sausage)

Preheat the oven to 325° F. Puncture each bratwurst with a pin in several places. Lightly oil a large skillet (we have 3 skillets going at once) and heat over medium heat until hot but not smoking. Add the bratwurst and cook, turning often with tongs, until bratwurst is brown on all sides, about 5 minutes. Place bratwurst in a baking dish, pour in the juices from the skillet, place dish in the oven, and cook, uncovered, until no redness shows when sausage is cut with knife, about 30 minutes.

    Meanwhile, place weisswurst and bauernwurst in a large 20-quart pot. Add enough water to cover. Heat to boiling and remove from heat. Cover and let stand 15 minutes.

    Serves 60.

Henderson Sauerkraut

  2 pounds lean bacon, diced
1½ cups (3 sticks) unsalted butter
 14 onions, diced
 28 red apples, peeled, cored, and diced
 28 19½-ounce cans prepared sauerkraut (we prefer
       Hengstenberg, which is wine-cured)
  3 tablespoons chopped fresh marjoram, or 1 tablespoon dried
 28 bay leaves*
 28 black peppercorns
  1 pound liverwurst (fresh, if available)
    Salt and freshly ground black pepper
  4 quarts apple juice
  5 tablespoons light brown sugar, lightly packed
1½ pounds lean double-smoked bacon, diced
  4 pounds carrots, peeled and sliced very thin

In a large (20-quart) soup pot, sauté the bacon over medium-high heat until golden. Add the butter and allow it to melt. Add the onions and cook until soft but not brown, about 5 minutes. Add the apples and cook until barely tender, about 5 minutes. Add the sauerkraut, marjoram, bay leaves, peppercorns, liverwurst, salt and pepper to taste, and 2 quarts of the apple juice. Heat to boiling, reduce heat, and simmer 2 hours. Add the remaining apple juice and the brown sugar; return to a simmer and cook 1 more hour. Add the smoked bacon and cook 45 minutes longer. Add the carrots and cook 15 minutes more. Serve hot.

Serves 60.

*We like the bay leaves and peppercorns floating free in our sauerkraut. If you don't, make a bouquet garni by tying bay leaves and peppercorns securely in a piece of cheesecloth.

TOP AND ABOVE: *The shiny new Northville fire truck and the old Henderson Farmall are on display.*

LEFT: *In wintertime, this truck lives on the windowsill of our New York City apartment, where Skitch can enjoy it during his jaunts to the city.*

The Firemen's Lunch

Boiled New Potatoes

The simplest dish of the day.

10 pounds small red potatoes
　Salt

Cook potatoes in boiling salted water until tender, about 20 minutes. Drain. Place in large serving bowls.

Serves 60.

Dark Chocolate Brownies

These delicious brownies bake slowly at a low temperature.

10 ounces (1½ cups) granulated sugar
　7 ounces (1 cup) light brown sugar, firmly packed
　4 eggs
　7 ounces (2 sticks less 2 tablespoons) unsalted butter, melted
　1 teaspoon vanilla extract
　5 ounces (1 cup) all-purpose flour
　3 ounces (¾ cup plus 2½ tablespoons) cocoa
　　Pinch of salt

Preheat oven to 275° F. Butter a 10 x 16-inch baking pan. Combine the sugars and eggs in the top of a double boiler; stir over simmering water until dissolved. Combine sugar mixture, melted butter, and vanilla in a large bowl; mix well.

　Sift the flour, cocoa, and salt together; stir into sugar mixture. Pour batter into a prepared pan. Bake until a sharp knife inserted in the center comes out clean, about 1 hour. Cool. Cut into 2-inch squares.

Makes about 40 brownies.

The Firemen's Lunch

187

INDEX